THE FRAME BOOK

Contemporary Design with Traditional and Modern Methods and Materials

THELMA R. NEWMAN
JAY HARTLEY NEWMAN
LEE SCOTT NEWMAN

Crown Publishers, Inc., New York

PREFACE AND ACKNOWLEDGMENTS

Frame making takes precise skill, as anyone who has attempted to cut a 45° angle in wood knows. Nevertheless, making frames is not difficult when the ways of craftsmanship shown within are followed. Anyone, with simple, basic tools, can make a frame. What distinguishes any old frame, however, from an outstanding job, is imagination. That is why many processes shown are open-ended, to involve you and your own ideas. A frame should be a personal expression designed for each particular work of art.

Emphasis here is on the contemporary, in design and in employing new technology. For the first time in any frame-making book, steps are given in designing frames of acrylic. Here too the potential is enormous, awaiting your attempts with these easy-to-use materials.

Special thanks goes to Chris Binaris who, as a hobbyist, has demonstrated his professional prowess as a frame maker and to Joseph Forgione who helped us make a basic frame. Also, many thanks to all the companies that gave us specific help in using their materials; and to Norm Smith for a beautiful photo-processing job.

And as always, our deepest gratitude to Jack Newman, husband and father of the authors, who pitched in, in countless ways, to keep the book "rolling."

THELMA R. NEWMAN
JAY HARTLEY NEWMAN
LEE SCOTT NEWMAN

NOTE: *All photographs by the authors, unless otherwise stated.*

© 1974 by Thelma R. Newman, Jay Hartley Newman, Lee Scott Newman

Library of Congress Catalog Card Number: 73-85858
ISBN: 0-517-513838
ISBN: 0-517-514273 pbk

Printed in the United States of America
Published simultaneously in Canada by
General Publishing Company Limited
Designed by Shari de Miskey and Deborah Daly

Fifth Printing, September, 1976

CONTENTS

The earliest frames grew out of architectural components. Paintings on wood required strong reinforcement, which became the frame. This tempera on wood by Sasetta dates back to the early fifteenth century. Courtesy: The Metropolitan Museum of Art, gift of George Blumenthal

1
THE FRAME— PAST AND PRESENT

Definition

A frame is a delineator, a definer. It outlines and encloses and in doing so helps to describe its contents which is usually a work of art. Like the setting of a play, a frame helps to dramatize the star's presence. As in a stage design, depending on its scale and proportion, mood and style, a frame can also upstage its contents by attracting all attention to itself. When functioning at its best, a frame can be a work of art, in the service of a work of art, setting its contents apart, raising it to prominence as a floral bower frames the bride and groom, as a doorway frames an entrance to a home or room, inviting one to enter. It delineates and establishes a reference point and visually forces a focus on one aspect, which in effect frames a scene into a picture.

History

The earliest frames were really suggestions of frames—like the monumental arch framing and focusing on one aspect of an avenue. A bas-relief, mosaic, or fresco usually was framed with a suggestion of a border made of the same material. A linear outline suggesting a border becomes a frame of mosaic for a mosaic. Wall areas defined by wall and ceiling supports became natural frames for wall paintings, just as the niches became part of the architectural vocabulary in defining spaces for sculpture or amphora. Indeed, the earliest frames in the fifteenth century were a pair of columns topped by an entablature, a concept that probably came from architectural details of buildings.

The implication for portability did not arise until there was a demand for paintings as a portable unit. This tempera and oil on wood, *The Retable of Le Cellier,* by Jean Bellegambe, reflects the architectural detail of a niche. Late fifteenth century. Courtesy: The Metropolitan Museum of Art, the Michael Friedsam Collection

The need for frames did not arise until the painting became a portable unit. Until then, at least to the Middle Ages, a painting was an integral part of architecture existing mainly on walls of buildings. The only exceptions were paintings on vases, boxes, and in portable, foldable niches. These early paintings were on wood and most likely the first frames were necessary to reinforce wooden panels and keep the works from warping. Necessarily, the first frame makers were painters who considered painting and frame as a whole. As demand for portable paintings increased, painters confined themselves to painting, and the need for fine frames launched a new craft.

Frame artisans gradually evolved into artists themselves and picture frames grew extraordinarily elaborate, particularly toward the end of the sixteenth century. The frame, often embedded with mother-of-pearl, stones, glass, and mirror, became more important than the picture itself. Elaborate carvings and investments flourished. The frame became an overadorned birthday cake surrounding a picture. By the seventeenth century, frame making was a recognized guild, an extension of cabinetmaking. The finest frames of this period were carved, gessoed, and gilded. But it was not long before a shortcut was found that looked much like the gessoed, gilded, hand-carved version. Frames were cast of plaster and gilded. This reduced time and price but extended the potential for gingerbread. By the end of the nineteenth century, artists revolted from the contrived ugliness of excessively embellished frames. The Impressionists constructed their own frames, using simple flat moldings. They tried to relate frame to picture. James Whistler was one who designed and made his own frames. Seurat even carried his pointillist background into the liner and onto the frame.

Frame artisans gradually evolved into artists themselves and picture frames grew extraordinarily elaborate as illustrated in this French gilded wood frame of the seventeenth century (period of Louis XVI). Courtesy: The Metropolitan Museum of Art, gift of J. Pierpont Morgan

By the seventeenth century, frame making was recognized as a guild. The finest frames were carved, gessoed, and gilded as in this Dutch seventeenth-century example that becomes at once a superelaborate history and a bas relief. Courtesy: The Metropolitan Museum of Art, gift of J. Pierpont Morgan

Elaborate carvings and investments suffered no constraints. This late seventeenth-century or early eighteenth-century French frame of carved wood, gessoed and gilded, later had counterparts that were cast of plaster, coated with gesso, and gilded. Courtesy: The Metropolitan Museum of Art, gift of J. Pierpont Morgan

The Frame

The frame can *be* many different forms. It can be as small as an inch or huge; it can take any shape—oblong, square, round, oval, hexagonal, and three-dimensional, be any color and be made of almost any solid material from tape to precious metal. As a presentation form, the frame can be attached to a wall, act as a divider between areas, or be freestanding and sit on a table. A frame can stand away from its contents or blend invisibly with the work of art.

DESIGN

Designwise there are no absolutes, no clear-cut rights and wrongs as to what a frame should be. Perhaps the only universals are that a frame should *blend with the style* of the work of art being presented (this does not mean that it should be the same style or period); and that, in size, it should be *in proportion to the work of art,* and not overpower it, or underdefine it.

The reasons for a frame are to focus vision and to limit the edges or to contain a volume—to define the "life" space around a work of art. In doing so, a frame should reinforce significant elements, such as texture and color. It can do this by repetition of common elements of color, texture, and pattern or by mildly contrasting with these elements. For example, a hard, glossy surface may be dramatized by a mat of light absorbing material such as velour, velvet, or felt. In harmonizing with a piece, a frame should help vision to linger. Its existence should be felt—not with as strong psychological power as the bars on a prison window, but rather as the bower around a bride and groom.

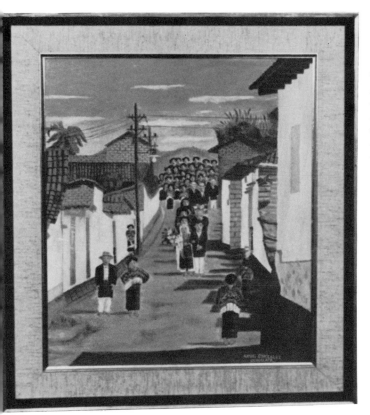

There are no clear-cut rights and wrongs as to what a frame should be. Perhaps one universal is that the frame should blend with the style of the work as in this Guatemalan primitive by Angel Gonzalez.

Another universal is that a frame should be in proportion to the work of art, and not overpower it or underdefine it. This is a cast aluminum frame with a light beige silk mat. The serigraph is by Vasarely.

A frame should reinforce significant elements, such as color. It can also mildly contrast with these elements. A combination frame defines an oil painting of "Jack" by Thelma R. Newman.

Each work of art has weight and quality which are not measurable in other terms, but reflect aesthetic sensibility. For example, a large, boldly contrasted peasant scene, expressed with bright colors and with roughly textured brush-strokes, could effectively be framed with roughhewn, weathered, sturdy, butt-joined wood, whereas a fine ink drawing needs a more delicate, narrower definition, perhaps even in passe-partout style, which is merely a tape binding around the mounting.

More generally, though, always with room for exceptions, a picture with a three-dimensional effect usually looks best with a molding that slants inward toward the composition, whereas a composition that is flat appears more successful with a flat molding or one that slants toward the wall. Similarly, a picture with dynamic movement requires a heavier frame to "contain" it.

Mood is also important. Fanciful subjects usually permit more inventiveness and license than hard-edged geometric subjects. Some geometric paintings look better without any frame at all.

The color of a frame should most often reveal something about the material it is made of. Wood grain, if attractive, should show through the protective finish. If the grain is nondescript, then lacquer, leafing, gesso, or paint can give it color or character. Likewise, metal should look like metal, plastic like plastic. More specifically, warm-toned pictures should have warm-toned frames, e.g., golds and warm browns, while cool-toned pictures look best with silvery or cool hues.

INSERTS

Inserts such as liners and mats can provide a soft transition between subtle aspects of a picture and the color of a frame. This can be accomplished by mats that accentuate colors in a picture, reinforce textures, or dramatize them with contrast. Cautions are necessary here, because very roughly textured mats such as rough burlap or Japanese grass cloth might drain subtly from delicate details by overpowering them. Usually, the most usable liners are made of linen, silk, or mat board. Velvet is popular but should be used sparingly with flat, delicate pieces. Perhaps the best use of velvet is to surround glossy or metallic components.

Inserts such as liners and mats can provide a soft transition between subtle aspects of a picture and the color of a frame. A detail of a painting by Jane Bearman. Frame by Sol Frances.

Proportion among elements is significant. Here is part one of a study in relationships of a brilliant color photo with its mats. This is a basic light gray mat.

A black mat is superimposed over the gray.

Here more prominence is given to the black outline. Later a plastic-metal-type frame will be added. See Chapter 5.

A dark gray mat is added. Note that the black edge is narrower here than in the next photo.

Papier-mâché was used to redesign an atrocious old frame.

◄

A combed gesso finish refurbishes an ordinary oak frame. Its linen mat and Japanese block printed paper as a countermount transform the Mexican bark paper fetish forms into something very special.

The original wooden frame around Philip Moore's painting did nothing for the piece. An acrylic frame was constructed to fit over the old frame.

Contrasting materials and using textures and colors to dramatize are important in frame making. Sylvia Massey's cast polyester head, a shiny piece, is contrasted by a velvet mat mount and defined by a gold leaf frame.

Novelty frames can be made of a wide variety of materials, such as ceramic, papier-mâché, leather.

A double frame becomes a shadow box for the Ecuadorian bread figure and Mexican beaded collar.

There are no hard-and-fast rules in frame making. Here is one that breaks away from basic concepts—an antique Spanish silver repoussé frame encloses a Guatemalan wedding veil. Both are bold and attention-getting. But it works!

A liner and single frame were used to define this bead and oil painting by Buramoih.

Ordinarily, round frames cannot be made easily by the craftsman, or even the professional frame maker. But with a new plastic-clad metal stripping, striking frames such as this one are possible and can be constructed in just minutes.

Mats and mounts come in a wide variety of colors, textures, and materials. Some are shown here.

The mat and double frame function as an integral part of this block print on fabric.

PROPORTION

Proportion among mat, liner, and frame is another element of design that must be considered. One rule is that these parts should not be of equal width. Repetition of widths is monotonous and redundant. There is a tendency today to use two or more liners that look like a ziggurat of wood causing the liners to assume more importance than the work that is being framed. In a small picture the mat should be not much more than 3″ wide, and in large pictures matting should have a 5″ maximum width. Of course, there are exceptions. One that comes to mind is a bright dominant three-dimensional object that demands a containing form larger than 3″–5″. Usually, wider mats cease being functional and become merely decorative and self-important.

Perhaps the most common crimes against good frame design are to trim a picture to fit a frame, to pick a color of mat because it matches a piece of furniture, and to enlarge a frame to fill a wall area.

ENVIRONMENT

Environment also can be significant in complementing a good job, or in minimizing what would have been an effective job of framing. For example, a busy floral wallpaper background usually is so overpowering that only the boldest composition with very dark and/or strong colors can compete. Contrasting colored wall covering, on the other hand, can make a piece stand out, whereas harmonizing wall coverings blend with a composition and psychologically appear to reduce its size. Passe-partout mounting also tends to marry a picture to a wall, particularly if the binding is the same color as the background.

When grouped, pictures should have some relationship to one another—it may be color, position, subject, and so on. In this, the frame molding is the same and the position shares a common invisible line between them.

These two molas from San Blas Island, Panama, are mounted in a frame with liner and another frame within. A natural cork panel on the background "ties" the two into a single unit.

Many pictures can be spaced to fill a wall. These cover an area of about 18 feet. All are related in style—primitive paintings; in the use of bright colors; and in a common color of the frames, black with gold trim; and in the use of light beige liners. Yet each frame is different.

Several pictures can be spaced to fill a wall area and, balanced with furniture elements, become a center of interest in a room. This kind of organization can be formally arranged with a central unit and duplicate-sized units on each side. Or it can be informally arranged, shifting the imaginary fulcrum to one side and thereby balancing a large area against a cluster of smaller units, which is more dynamic. There is a way to unify divergent parts by extending imaginary lines in the mind's eye from the perimeters of frames or mats and using that "edge" as a boundary for another picture (see diagram). These imaginary lines form a unifying grid that coordinates elements into a cohesive whole.

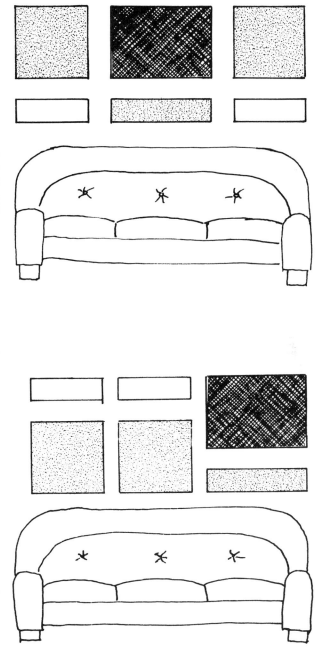

A formal, symmetrical arrangement of frames (texture indicates value—how light or dark a picture is). Although neat, the arrangement is static and dull.

This is an attempt at asymmetrical or informal balance. It does not work because the frames on the right suggest too heavy (dark) values and throw the arrangement off. If the larger dark painting were of a lighter color, it would create a balanced effect.

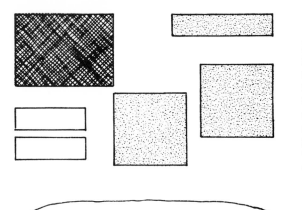

Here is another informal or asymmetrically balanced arrangement using the same elements as in the other two arrangements. It works in this organization because space, size, and color (with value) are considered. All parts appear to hold together as a unit because of an invisible grid of lines which the next diagram makes visible.

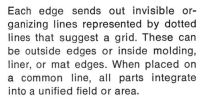

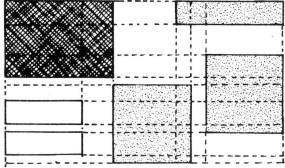

Each edge sends out invisible organizing lines represented by dotted lines that suggest a grid. These can be outside edges or inside molding, liner, or mat edges. When placed on a common line, all parts integrate into a unified field or area.

HANGING

Most people hang pictures too high on the wall. The best formula to use when making this decision is to consider whether people will be standing or sitting when looking at the framed piece. Most pictures should be hung at eye level, particularly small ones. The best location for a picture is in a position where there is the broadest visibility or where vision is focused, as at the end of a hallway. Certainly, works of art should not be hung over heat, over a fireplace, or in the path of dirt-carrying drafts of hot air.

Once upon a time, pictures hung from covered wires strung from picture moldings near the ceiling, and they glanced down at you at an angle. Although the style yet may return, it is recommended that it is less distracting for picture hooks to remain invisible behind the frame. Of course, do not use nails for hanging that would protrude and possibly puncture your work of art. It is best to hang medium-sized and large pictures on two picture hooks. (The hooks don't have to be exactly the same height.) Framed pieces do not shift that way, and the weight is better distributed. Check picture hooks periodically for loosening.

LIGHT

Light is another important element of the environment. It influences shape, depth, color. Glass in a frame can reflect light and nearly obliterate the contents of a frame. (Nonreflective glass helps solve that problem.) One should be concerned, therefore, about light sources, ways to shield light, funnel it, deflect it, bounce it, and avoid annoying reflections.

The best light is natural light. But harsh unfiltered sunlight can destroy some fabrics and colors. Overhead, shielded fluorescent lights can approximate sunlight in effectiveness, as can skylights and spotlights in or on a ceiling. As a last resort, a light over a picture can be used, but it looks pretentious. Rays of light usually fan down onto a picture, and if it is an oil painting, light creates a glare on some parts, leaving other areas in darkness. The total effect is unnatural.

Traditions of Frames

There are traditions in framing that have been proved by time and that have set standards for framing, such as when to use glass or mats, and so on. These are generalizations, again, where departures are permissible after one considers alternatives.

OIL PAINTINGS: The frame has to be mechanically strong to contain the wooden stretcher and keep it from warping. No glass or mat is used, but sometimes liners are employed.

WATERCOLORS: Frames are shallower and usually narrower. Medium to wide mats (3″–5″ and less) are used.

PASTELS: Frames are similar to watercolors, but spacers or liners should be used to keep the glass from touching the chalky surface.

GOUACHE: These are similar to watercolors but usually painted with stronger, more opaque colors; therefore a heavier frame can be used. Glass and mat are also recommended.

GRAPHICS (drawings and prints such as etchings, lithographs, and so on): Usually narrow wooden or metal moldings are used. Mats are soft, off-white. The important plate mark on the print should *not* be hidden by the mat. Glass or plastic is used to protect it.

PHOTOGRAPHY: Frames usually are narrow, but can vary from no frame, where the print is mounted without any borders on a block of wood or plastic foam, to more important widths. When framed, mats and glass are used. In either case, the photo print is usually rubber cemented or heat sealed to a rigid mounting board to keep the edges from curling.

REPRODUCTIONS: Color, texture, and size usually determine whether the surface needs protection with glass. If the surface has a linenlike texture and is varnished, glass is not necessary. Framing of this type is usually in the style of oil paintings.

THREE-DIMENSIONAL OBJECTS: If the three-dimensional form can be mounted, framing probably would best be accomplished in a double, or shadow-box-like frame that is fronted with glass. A freestanding form should be boxed in an acrylic boxlike mounting over a base that permits viewing from all directions.

MIRRORS: If the mirror is decorative, framing probably would be in the style of the furnishings because a decorative mirror is more like a piece of furniture. A functional mirror should have a more simple, less distracting frame so that the image of the moment can be enjoyed.

MOUNTING
AND
MATTING

For both aesthetic and practical purposes, many objects should be mounted before framing. Prints, old papers, drawings, and photographs are often too fragile or too thin to be framed without additional support. Mounting usually supplies a substantial backing to make framing easier and more effective.

Mounting may be used in two basic ways. The mounting board may be a special piece of mat board which will then be framed with the attached print or photograph. Or the mounting surface may be used solely to hold the work in position, flat and with good support. In the latter case, mat used as a background will usually be cut after mounting to fit properly and finish the piece for framing.

Kinds of Mount Boards

Mount boards are available in a large variety of weights, thicknesses, sizes, textures, and stiffnesses. The two most common mounts are temlock and Upson board. Both are available in the standard 4′ × 8′ size. Temlock, a refined wallboard, is ⅜″ thick and is slightly porous. Upson board is 3/16″ thick and very rigid and solid. In addition, regular mat board is used for mounting. Extrathick mat board, illustration board, and chipboard (bookbinder's board) are also widely used. Masonite, plasterboard, and plywood find application on occasion, but, for most purposes, the last three are somewhat thick and heavy.

The newest—and possibly the best—mounting material is foam core board manufactured by several companies and now widely available. This is a sandwich of Styrofoam laminated between two sheets of white oaktag or kraft paper. This board is rigid and it is extremely lightweight. Although it costs more than some

Mounting and matting boards come in a large variety of textures, patterns, and colors. The boards shown here include metallics, boards in mat colors, grass cloth, linen, burlap, silk, pebbled, cork, and flocked mats.

of the other choices, it has the virtue of being easy to cut in addition to being very light and rigid. Because of these factors, it often saves a great deal of time and labor.

The choice of which kind of board to use will depend on what you are mounting. A large piece should always be mounted on a thick piece of board. This is true of heavy works as well. The reason for this is that the mount should always serve to keep the item being framed flat and free from warpage. A thin board over a large area will tend to warp because of changes in humidity and temperature that will not affect thicker boards as much, particularly if the frame provides some support. If there is a choice to be made, always err on the side of too thick a mounting background than on the side of too thin.

Another consideration is how the mount fits into the scheme of framing for a particular object. If you are mounting a photograph, you may not intend to add a beveled mat after mounting; in that case, choose a fine white or colored mat board that will enhance the mounted picture. A gray chipboard would hardly be suitable in this case. But if you fully expect to use the mount only as a backing, the appearance does not matter.

Something to consider when working with these materials is the possibility of a combination of mountings and mats. A little glue will go a long way toward creating original frames. You might consider mounting a fine print on a piece of gold or colored paper, adhering that paper to a basic mount (this is called a countermount), and then adding a mat. Patterned papers of special design, hand-marbled, painted papers, even newspaper or collage may enhance certain subjects. The possibilities are endless; something can be devised to suit any subject.

Mounting Techniques

Once you have decided which mount or combination of mounts will best suit your subject, there are several means of attaching the subject to the board. One of the most difficult methods is the use of the *wet mount*. This technique is usually reserved for damaged, bent, or crumpled objects. It is of little value here, belonging more to the vocabulary of the restorer than the custom framer.

The two other methods—*dry mounting* and *adhesive mounting*—are both easy and extremely practical techniques for permanently bonding subjects to the mount in preparation for framing.

DRY MOUNTING

The dry mount utilizes a special paper that has been coated with a plastic adhesive which is activated by the application of heat and pressure. This paper is called the mounting tissue.

In the dry mount process, after measuring for placement, the tissue is attached to the mounting board in a few places with a tacking iron (or a household iron); the subject is laid over the tissue, and the sandwich of mounting board, tissue, and subject is placed in a dry-mounting press or is thoroughly heated and bonded with an iron supplying even pressure.

This technique is most often employed with photographs, small prints, and, on occasion, fabrics where heat will not cause any damage. Dry mounting assures that the subject will be firmly bonded to its mount for many years. It keeps the edges from curling, too.

ADHESIVE MOUNTING

Adhesive mounting is an alternative to dry mounting that many custom framers find attractive because it offers all of the advantages while eliminating the need for a special press or heat.

The basic technique can be described quite simply as gluing the subject to the mount. There are many kinds of glues that may be used for this purpose. The traditional kinds—the basic all-purpose white glue, and animal glues—are still very effective and extremely permanent. But newer alternatives also have their merits. In particular, the spray rubber cements, like Spra-ment Adhesive, bond very securely. And sheets of double-stick film for attaching papers, plastics, and photographs have many applications for the framer.

To use the spray cements, spray the mounting surface evenly with the cement, allow it to dry until very tacky, and then firmly press your subject down. To be certain that you lay the subject without creating any wrinkles, hold the paper or cloth up at each end, set the belly down, and press down each end from the center of the sheet outward.

The adhesive film works slightly differently; most of the films are backed on each side by waxed paper. First, cut the papered film to the proper size. Peel the waxed paper off one side, and press it firmly onto the mounting board. Then peel the other side, and carefully press down your photo or print. These adhesives are very strong, and they will not allow you to peel up the subject, so be certain that you have laid it down properly the first time. If necessary, use penciled rules to check for the proper alignment.

ADHESIVE MOUNTING

Adhesive mountings for photographs, small prints, posters, and cards, besides being very practical, keep edges from curling. The sheet of double-stick film shown here offers a successful alternative to the traditional dry mount which requires the application of heat. The first step in this process is to peel away the paper from one side of the film. Carefully press the film—sticky side down—onto the mounting surface. The best technique is to hold the film with one hand and smooth it down with the other. This will help to avoid wrinkles and air bubbles which would destroy the effect.

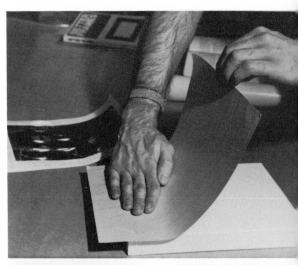

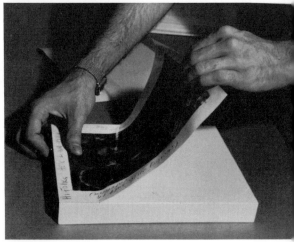

Once the film has been properly laid, turn the mounting surface upside down and trim away the excess with a sharp knife. Remove the other facing paper and smooth on the photograph bubble free. Once again, be careful. Work slowly and be certain that your artwork has been aligned correctly. This film is so tacky that most papers will rip if you try to remove them.

A beveled mat was added to set off the photograph. The frame is a commercial one consisting of a plastic box with white cardboard insert.

Mounting boards can become an integral part of the frame as well. In this example, a framed *mola* was attached with adhesive to a mounting board covered with burlap. A thick piece of board was necessary to prevent warpage.

THE MAT AND MOUNT AS FRAME

This series shows the possibility of using a mat-mount as a freestanding frame for a small picture. Begin with four pieces of cardboard of the same size, and enough bookbinding cloth to cover one side of each. Cut windows in two pieces of the board to the size you need for your pictures.

Adhere the cardboard with PVA onto the cloth, as shown here. Clip and miter the corners, and fold them back, around the cardboard. In the frame area cut out a small piece so that this part can be folded back as well.

Attach two pieces of decorative paper on the hinged booklike part and then on three sides glue the frames to the decorative paper. One area should be unattached so that a picture can be slid into place.

Backing for freestanding frames can serve a dual purpose: support for the art work and a backing for the frame. These two examples present the basic idea for you to expand upon.

Matting

Mounting, of course, is an important step in the framing process. But it is only one of several. After your subject has been mounted, you will often want to add the *mat* that protects your mounted (or unmounted) subject from direct contact with the glass of the frame. In this sense—the need to protect the work of art from direct pressure—the matting serves a very utilitarian purpose. But the mat is far more important today as the flexible and effective means of accenting and focusing our attention on the subject within the frame.

MOUNTING CUTOUTS ON GLASS AND ACRYLIC
Black and white and colored prints can be mounted on glass and acrylic directly and permanently. It is best to cut the prints into small units, but this one was not difficult to handle so it was left in one piece. These are German silhouettes cut from very thin black paper. They are to be mounted on glass and framed. The glass is cleaned with alcohol to dissolve grease and re-remove fingermarks. Soap and water can also be used.

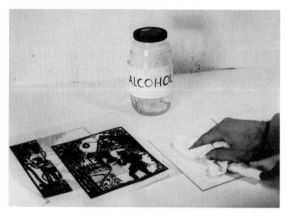

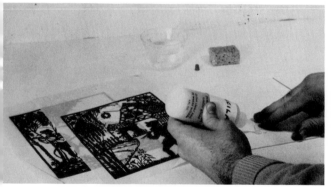

Mucilage (Harrower House) was used because it adheres well to glass. To slow the drying of the glue, you can add one-quarter teaspoon of glycerine to one-quarter cup of mucilage. Apply the glue to the glass and spread thin with your fingers.

Place the picture face up on a piece of waxed paper. Then lift the waxed paper with print, turn it over and, at the same time, carefully press the print against the glass at the top and work toward the bottom. Peel away the waxed paper. Press the silhouette with your fingers and a sponge to make certain that all parts are firmly and completely adhered. Turn the glass over to see whether air bubbles are trapped. If they are, carefully work them out.

Clean away the glue from open areas with sponge and water. Be careful not to disturb delicate sections. If stubborn glue spots remain, use a cotton swab and some warm vinegar and water to clean them away.

The completed pieces were backed with a pearlized Styrofoam "paper," the kind used as place mats on airline trays. It sticks to the glass and paper without glue. Then the pieces were framed. The decorative hardware may or may not be used for hanging. This and other techniques for mounting/decoupage are detailed in *Contemporary Decoupage* by Thelma R. Newman.

Decoupage allows the framer to create built-in matlike borders for frames very easily. The combination of acrylic mirror (which is available from most plastics' suppliers and some glaziers) and acrylic (polymer) emulsion works especially well. Here acrylic emulsion is being brushed onto the surface of the mirror, for one strip at a time. Other sections of paper are held in place temporarily with plastic putty.

Wrapping paper was cut into strips with corners mitered to fit precisely. To affix the paper to the mirror start at one end and work out bubbles with finger pressure as more and more of the strip is attached. Follow the same procedure all around, attaching colored paper strips and embossed gold stripping. For the gold stripping, which is stiffer, apply acrylic emulsion to both surfaces—mirror and back of stripping—before affixing. Use a brayer lightly if necessary to set the trim in place.

After all the paper has been adhered, coat the paper surfaces with four coats of acrylic emulsion. Wait for each coat to dry before applying the next, and remove any emulsion from the mirror face.

The mirror is framed in an aluminum strip frame. Foam core board was glued to the back of the mirror to make up the one inch depth necessary to fit the mirror securely into the frame.

DESIGN CONSIDERATIONS

The first element in the selection of a mat is size. The proportion of matting in relation to both subject and frame is crucial. As a general rule of thumb, the dimensions of a mat should never be less than 2½" on the side and top, and 3" on the bottom unless, of course, the subject is very small. Why the difference in the width of the bottom? The framer must correct for a perceptual illusion. You can test this out yourself. Cut a piece of mat or paper with all sides the same width, and place this over a likely subject, above eye level. What is the result? Most likely the picture will seem to be falling out of the frame. This results from the inability of the eye to judge properly the vertical distance between frame and picture center. Because we realize this, the addition of a half inch (or even more if the mat is to create a larger border) on the bottom dimension corrects our inaccurate perception and produces a result we find pleasing rather than disconcerting. But if the picture is to be hung at eye level, this illusion is not created; therefore it is unnecessary to have a larger margin at the base.

Aside from this correction, the size of the mat may vary greatly. From the lower limit, you may extend the size of the mat until, in some cases, the mat is larger than the print itself. Everything depends on what is being framed. A very strong subject may require a large mat of a related or contrasting color and texture. A delicate object can be destroyed by strong contrast, and needs a subtle, plain mat. Skill in framing results from your own ability to perceive what will best focus the viewer's eye. And the skillful use of mats plays no small part in this process.

KINDS OF MATS

Mats offer the custom framer a great range. To begin with, there are hundreds of colors of commercially manufactured mats. In addition to colors, most manufacturers also make a range of metallic mat boards, and some even sell double-sided boards so that the framer has a choice of two colors with each board.

Just as there is a range of colors, mats offer a great variety of texture, too. Linen, burlap, silk, pebbled, smooth, cork, velvet, are all available in many qualities and colors. And, of course, the framer has the final alternative of making his own cloth-covered mats with yardage and mat base.

The basic materials for mat cutting and beveling are shown here. A T square or right angle, straightedge, pencil, eraser, razor knife, and Dexter mat cutter are pictured. Underneath is a sheet of Neolite purchased from a shoe maker. The Neolite is an excellent base that keeps knives from dulling, yet provides enough resistance for cutting.

CUTTING A MAT

An important aspect of the mat is the beveled edge. This touch does so much for the continuity of a frame that it is foolish to learn the framing skill without learning how to bevel mat edges. The bevel funnels vision in toward the picture.

At one point, this single aspect of the craft was a skill all its own. Matmakers took a special—and not undeserved—pride in their ability to cut a perfectly beveled mat. One of the high points of our research was witnessing something which we can only recount here: the master mat cutter who cut a perfect oval with only a pencil line to guide him—a testament to his practice and skill. For the beginning craftsman, and, in fact, for the practicing professional, skillful beveling need not be the reward of endless practice, because the basic technique is easily learned with modern tools.

The framer today most often uses a steel ruler and a razor knife. As shown later in this chapter, the mat is cut from its back. Using the steel rule as a guide, the razor knife is drawn slowly and evenly down the mat. When all four sides have been cut, the center piece will fall out cleanly (if it does not, simply cut the attached paper with care using a thin razor blade). This is the basic practice. The steel rule, while an expensive tool, is useful and long-lasting.

A print by artist Jane Beerman is first placed on a sheet of mat board to decide upon the proper size of the mount. Measure the size to allow for appropriate borders.

Cut the mount on a paper cutter, or cut it with a knife. Just be certain that your mount is perfectly squared at the corners.

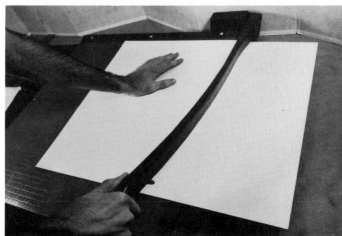

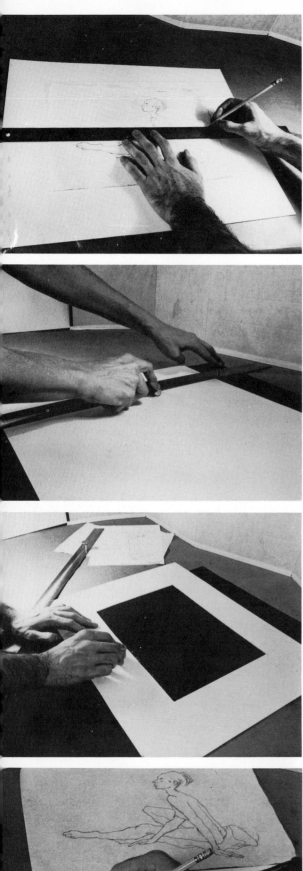

After the mount has been cut, the print is once again placed on it and centered. It is then measured for the beveled mat opening which will be placed on top. The mat should cover the edges of the print, and it should be of proportions which will enhance the work of art. If the print has a plate mark, the mark should show as well as the print number and artist's signature.

Traditionally, mats are beveled from the back. The tools shown here are the ANKER EDGE, a steel rule which can be clamped onto the edge of a table, and an angled razor knife which comes with the ANKER EDGE. By holding the steel rule firmly in place along the cutting line and smoothly drawing the razor knife toward you, a perfect beveled edge results. The secret here is that an angled roller holds the knife at the proper angle for cutting. Although the cutting surface was a piece of Neolite, newspapers or composition board may also be used to cut on.

When all four sides have been cut the center window will fall out. Turn the mat over and remove any smudges or pencil marks with a Pink Pearl eraser.

Place the mat over the mounting board and lightly mark the mount at each corner. The marks will serve as guides when tacking on your art work.

Use rubber cement to tack on the print in several spots just to hold it in place.

Rubber cement is brushed onto the top edge of the mounting board . . .

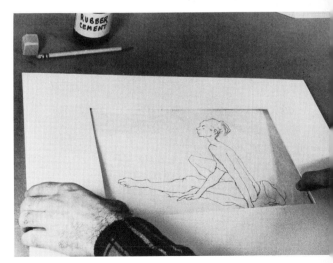

. . . and the mat is placed over the print and pressed down firmly. The finished frame, which illustrates the passe-partout process, appears in Chapter 3.

There are two other methods of getting perfect bevels. The first is by far the best, and it calls for the use of a very expensive Bainbridge mat cutter. This is a precision tool made and sold by Bainbridge only. But since this is an expensive investment, many framers have started using a hand beveler first, the Dexter mat cutter. Inexpensive and very well engineered, this mat cutter cuts from the front of the mat, and combines relatively low cost with good results. Two techniques for cutting a beveled mat are shown on these pages.

In addition to the traditional beveled steel rule and the ANKER EDGE, the Dexter mat cutter offers the frame maker a versatile mat-cutting tool. Because it is relatively inexpensive and very easy and effective to use, this tool might be a good investment. Unlike other techniques, the Dexter cuts mats from the front. It is only necessary to outline your window, align the T square, and push the tool along without stopping. Smoothness is the operative word in all mat cutting. Jolts, stops, and starts produce ragged edges.

Mats can be combined, as they are here. Different colors, in this case off white, black, and gray, produce striking results. Attach mats with a polyvinyl acetate (PVA), white glue.

Place the mats together carefully and press them together firmly.

A convenient system of matting involves the use of a tape "hinge." Wide masking tape is folded and half is pressed onto the mount. In this case a photograph has already been mounted.

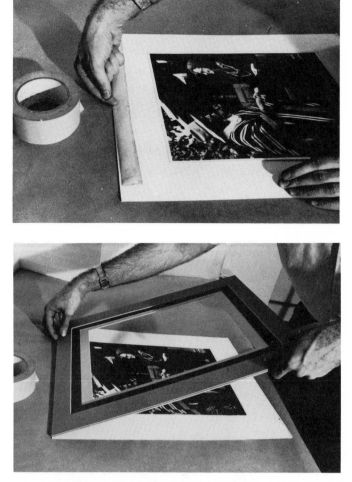

The mats are then placed on top of the mount, and the other half of the masking tape adheres to the mat.

The result is a hinge which holds mat and mount together, and allows easy access to the art work for adjustment or removal. The completed frame using this matting system is illustrated in Chapter 5 on Plastics.

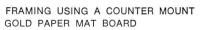

FRAMING USING A COUNTER MOUNT
GOLD PAPER MAT BOARD

Beginning with a piece of gold paper mat board, a rectangle slightly larger than the dimensions of a small Chinese print was centered and marked in pencil.

A bead of white glue was squeezed onto the back of the print and smoothed with a finger. The artwork was carefully centered and pressed into place on the gold mounting.

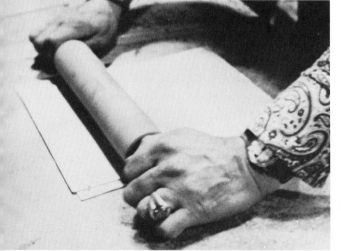

To secure it firmly, a piece of paper was placed over the print, and a rolling pin was used to apply firm, even pressure and to assure a solid bond.

This illustrates the use of an angled metal ruler and a razor knife. The beveled edge of the steel rule guides the razor. Here, a mat is being cut from the back to accent our print.

When beveling an edge you must always begin slightly beyond the line which shows the exact dimension of the window. In case you underestimate (and it is clearly better to underestimate than to overestimate) use a single-edged razor to cut the corners and finish the job cleanly. Rough edges may be smoothed by sanding them lightly with fine sandpaper. This will remove burrs.

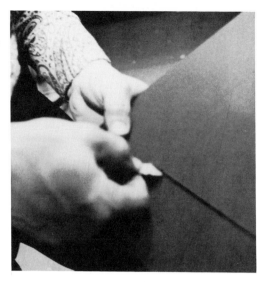

The black mat was then glued to the gold mounting, leaving a narrow, elegant border of gold paper around the print. White glue was used.

If necessary, the edges may be trimmed afterwards the way master frame maker Chris Benaris shows here. Any stray pencil marks or smudges should be removed with a Pink Pearl eraser. Be especially careful when working with black matboards. They will show erasures, if you press too hard or erase too long.

COVERING A MAT

Although a large range of colors, cloths, and textures are available to the framer, you may still want to cover your own mats with cloth. On some occasions this may be because you simply cannot find the proper color or fabric already matted. At other times, after you have discovered how easy and pleasurable the process is, your attempts to achieve the perfectly crafted frame will demand this additional personal touch.

For a covered mat, begin with a piece of chipboard, mat board, or foam core. Check first to make certain that your fabric is not so sheer that the color of the board will show through. If it does, choose a color of board that will complement the cloth. The cloth should be a few inches wider than the board on each side (6″ on each dimension). The steps which follow are detailed photographically here. Basically, the framer must cut the window to the proper size—with a beveled edge, if possible. Paint the mat surface with glue; lay down and smooth out the cloth. Then slice corners so that cloth does not overlap and bunch up; cut and glue back the inside and outside edges. There is no need to become involved with the elaborate old-fashioned techniques of hot-gluing and pressing fabrics. Modern glues and methods are just as successful and attractive.

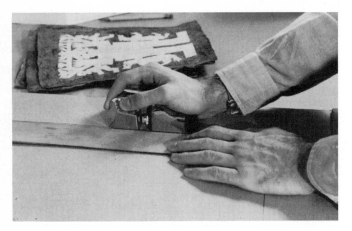

The Dexter mat cutter is used here to cut heavy chipboard which will be the base for a cloth-covered mat. The beveled edge provides a very fine touch to the finished product. Boards can be covered with almost any cloth—linen, silk, burlap, velvet, cotton, to name a few fabrics.

The best adhesive for attaching cloth to paperboards is a spray rubber cement. The cement should be sprayed evenly over the entire top surface.

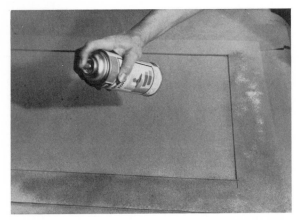

Rather than attempt to place the cloth over the board, the unwrinkled, newly pressed linen is spread on a clean table, and the chipboard is carefully placed on it and pressed down firmly.

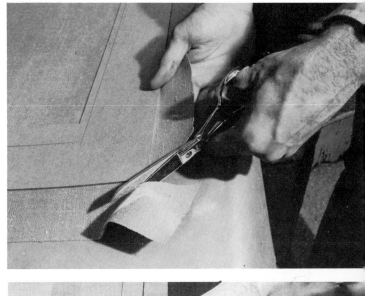

While the cement is setting, the corners may be cut away. The cloth need be only an inch and a half larger than the board on each side to accommodate the thickness of the chipboard. Cutting the corners will assure that no bulky overlaps will be obvious when the edges are glued back.

Leaving a border of an inch of cloth, cut a window in the cloth. This piece of fabric should be saved. It may be useful for another, smaller mat later on. Cut the inside border of cloth at a 45° angle at each corner. Use a sharp razor knife for all cuts to make certain that you do not pull any threads and cause the fabric to ravel.

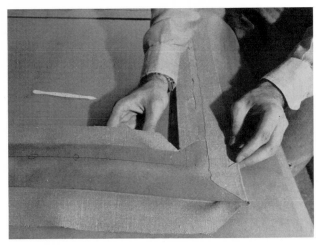

Spray the back of the mat board with rubber cement as well. In a continuous motion, pull and press down the borders of cloth so that they are adhered evenly to the back of the paperboard.

Using the same versatile rubber cement, a piece of patterned, printed, Japanese paper is adhered to a sheet of foam core which has been cut to size.

When all borders have been glued, turn the mat right side up and use a plastic burnishing tool or another blunt object to smooth down the cloth wherever air bubbles or separations appear. Few, if any, should be visible if the adhesive was applied evenly and the board was pressed down firmly in the first place.

As you can see here, the patterned paper forms an attractive backing for these Mexican bark figures. The linen mat accents this nicely. (The entire frame is shown in Chapter 4.)

A fine silk mat was used with this print by Vasarely. The texture and color of the fabric you choose can highlight artwork very effectively by picking up certain colors or by echoing a pattern.

THE MAT'S COUSIN—THE LINER

Not only can fabrics be incorporated into a framing process through mats, but you can apply the cloth to wood molding too. Cloth-covered molding, which is usually used in conjunction with an uncovered outer molding, is called a *liner*. While the construction end of liners' creation is the same as with basic frame making (shown in Chapter 3), the covering of molding with cloth to form the liner in the first place is akin to covering mats.

For example, raw painter's linen can be put on the surface of molding (the inner molding is also called the "insert") with the all-purpose white glue or rubber cement sprays. Linen can be glued to four separate pieces of molding after they have been cut to size or even before being cut. Or else the linen can be put on the molding after construction of the molding into a rectangular frame. To do it by the latter process, first cut the strips of linen to the length of each molding strip after constructing the insert frame, but before nailing this frame to the outer not-to-be-covered frame molding. Make them wide enough to cover the width of the molding just under the rabbet.

Cover the walls of the rabbet with the glue for one of the four sides. Press the linen to this rabbet with the linen edge even with the bottom edge of the rabbet. Cut the linen at its ends to follow diagonally along the mitered joints of the frame. Make certain there are no wrinkles or air pockets. Smear or spray glue onto the face and back of the molding and press down the linen. Do not apply too much glue or it will seep through the linen and look messy from the front. An alternative to glue is library paste which can be removed if the linen has been stained. After the linen has hardened onto the frame bar, use a metal ruler and razor knife to finely trim off the minor excess of linen which may go beyond the mitered joints onto the next molding bar. It is at this joint that the linen strips should match exactly with no overlap and no gaps, either. Repeat this process for all four sides of the insert frame to complete the liner. If you are having trouble getting the linen to lie perfectly flat on your liner, use a blunt tool like a bone burnisher or the back of a spoon to rub the insert until the linen adheres completely.

The alternative method for applying cloth to an insert frame to form a liner is to glue the linen to the wood strips before forming the strips into a frame. Cut the lengths of linen for each strip with an excess half an inch or so at each end. Glue as before, and also glue that overlap excess onto the mitered edges of the molding strips. Now proceed to join the molding strips as described in Chapter 3. This joining should be done before the other glue or paste has had much time to set. The product is usually much neater than the other method of applying linen. Both find important and regular use in the designing and making of frames, as we shall see.

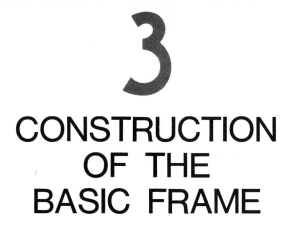

CONSTRUCTION
OF THE
BASIC FRAME

The techniques found in this chapter on making the essential frame are common to just about every frame that the hobbyist or frame maker will devise. Variations occur when you start using different moldings and combinations and when you apply different finishes to those moldings. In fact, once you have mastered the basic methods, your variations on the simple theme by your imagination and design preference should assume control of your product.

Types of moldings available for framing can be broken down into two main categories: picture frame moldings (made especially for framing and which have built-in rabbets) and builder's moldings (made for house trimming without rabbets). There are also frames made of found objects, and discoveries made in the attic and basement of old doorframes and window frames. If you add to these the many different ways of combining frames within frames—such as in liners and shadow boxes—the number of unique frames possible becomes extensive.

Lumber suppliers usually have a broader selection of moldings without rabbets (the indentation that holds the picture in place) than of special picture frame moldings. But since rabbets can easily be added onto the back of any molding frame, this should not deter the frame maker who is looking for a particular style such as plain, flat strips of wood.

The most basic frame-making technique, when used with imagination, taste, and skill, can complement any picture or object. Here a gold-leafed antique-finished frame combined with a flat, black velvet mat forms a handsome contrast to the shiny face of the polyester resin head by Sylvia Massey.

Again, this is just a single molding style which is measured, mitered, and joined to suit Joseph Demarais's collagraph.

CROSS SECTIONS OF VARIOUS MOLDINGS

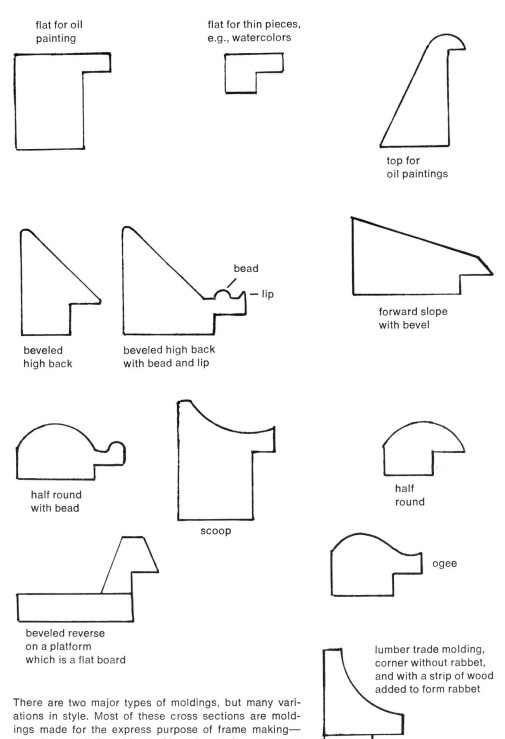

flat for oil
painting

flat for thin pieces,
e.g., watercolors

top for
oil paintings

beveled
high back

beveled high back
with bead and lip

bead

lip

forward slope
with bevel

half round
with bead

scoop

half
round

beveled reverse
on a platform
which is a flat board

ogee

lumber trade molding,
corner without rabbet,
and with a strip of wood
added to form rabbet

There are two major types of moldings, but many variations in style. Most of these cross sections are moldings made for the express purpose of frame making—they have built-in rabbets. Also shown, however, are builder's moldings (also called stripping or batten) to which a strip of wood must be added to create a rabbet. The rabbet helps to hold the framed object.

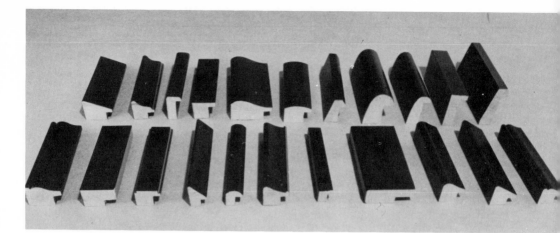

Picture frame moldings are available in a variety of bevels, curves, and flats, either already finished or plain for the self-finisher.

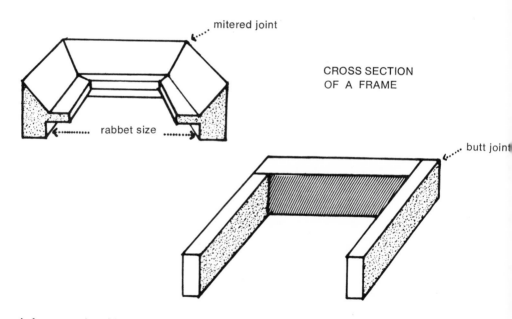

A frame made with butt joints requires no miter box or guillotine, since it is only made with 90° angle cuts. Butt-joined strips are also used most often as an addition to the back of builder's molding frames to serve as the rabbet. Also shown is a cross section of a frame using rabbeted molding. Notice the difference in width between its rabbet size and where the inner lip of the visible frame ends. This is an important consideration when measuring for a fit.

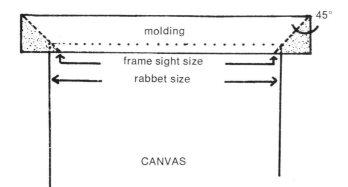

In measuring the molding, do take into consideration this difference between rabbet size and the frame sight size. The work being framed fits into the rabbet, so always measure along the inner edge of the rabbet and not along the outside edge of the molding. Notice also that the length of a piece of molding which will be mitered must be equal to the length of the picture size plus twice the width of the molding itself (to compensate for mitering).

Adding on a Rabbet to Builder's Molding

To adapt a lumber-trade molding to picture framing, strips of at least ¼″ wide and ⅜″ deep can be glued and/or nailed to the underside of the frame molding. Most rabbets need not be deeper than ¼″ to ½″ except when you are framing a canvas which is mounted on a stretcher. For convenience, you may choose to use standard ½″ × ¾″ parting strips as your regular rabbet-forming addition to builder's molding. These underside strips need not be mitered; their edges may be butt joined.

Measuring

Since so much of good frame making relies on accuracy of measurement, let us for a moment consider what and how to measure in preparing to cut and join moldings. Frame sizes are generally measured in two ways: *rabbet size* and *frame sight size*. The latter is the measure of a specific area of picture to be seen through the frame—the visible picture area. The rabbet size measures the larger opening at the back of the frame in which the entire picture or mat must sit. The rabbet size will always exceed the frame sight size by twice the width of the rabbet. This makes it possible for mats, mounts, glass, etc. to be snugly accommodated. Having the rabbet size larger than the frame sight size simply means that a lip of frame will overlap part of the picture and hold it in place.

Aside from considering the dangers of cropping out too much of a picture, the frame sight size is relatively unimportant in the mechanics of frame making. What is important, and what will continually be referred to in this book, is the rabbet size. If the shape formed by the molding's rabbet is too wide or narrow, the picture will not fit properly—being either too loose or too small.

Measurements, then, are of utmost importance, so continually recheck all lengths and angles as you make any frame or rabbet. Specifically, when using rabbet size measures, make these dimensions just a hair larger than the dimensions of the picture itself. An extra 1/16″ should be enough to allow the picture to slip in and out easily without being too loose. For example, if you want to frame an 18″ × 24″ picture, add on ⅛″ (1/16″ for each end of the strip) to both length and width, making the rabbet size 18⅛″ × 24⅛″. This leeway is often essential because, once you have cut a molding or made the rabbet and frame too small, there is no way of using that piece unless you plan to saw an end off your picture. If one isn't careful in measuring, when it comes time to complete the frame you may find yourself like the man who, finding one leg of a table too long, cuts it shorter and discovers that it is now too short, and so cuts down the other three legs too, but again finds the fourth leg too long, etc. etc.

Returning to the attachment of parting strips to builder's molding to make a rabbet, first measure the length and width of the picture to be framed, then add to this length the extra ⅛″ safety space. Cut the strips at straight angles (90°), and butt the ends to form your rectangle. Check at this point to be certain the picture will fit in this rabbet before going ahead and joining the strips to the frame.

Glue the four strips end to face (using Elmer's Glue-All or another white polyvinyl acetate glue) to form the rectangle in which the picture will later sit. The picture should fit snugly in this makeshift glued rabbet. Glue this rectangle to the back of the already completed frame which has been properly mitered, glued, and nailed together (as we will discuss later).

A few of the tools of the trade include a miter box (inexpensive model shown here with back saw and molding strip); assorted brads and finishing nails; medium-weight claw hammer; polyvinyl acetate (PVA) in squeeze container (that's an all-purpose white glue like Elmer's Glue-All or Sobo); an angle clamp (for holding glued mitered edges perfectly butted); a nail set for sinking nails below the surface of finished frames; a collapsible wooden ruler with metal edge (excellent for measuring molding and wood); and a metal ruler (the Stanley AR100 ruler shown here has a handy right angle in it).

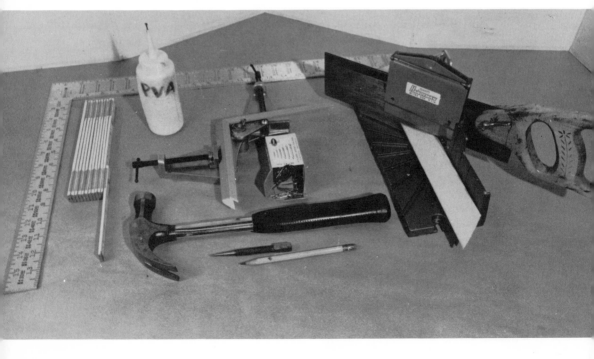

Tools of the Trade

There are a few essential tools for making a simple frame. Perhaps most important in the frame-making craft is the tool that cuts accurate, regular 45° angles. This may be a *miter box* and backsaw; hand or electric *guillotine* (or "chopper"); or even a *crosscut saw with protractor*.

Most popular is the miter box. It is in most cases the most expensive tool the frame maker will ever have to purchase. Stanley, for instance, makes a complete line of efficient, effective, and accurate miter boxes (nos. 60, 100, 115, and 150), all of which are good. If you plan to do much framing, the more expensive miter boxes can usually be expected to remain truer over time.

The hand or electric guillotine is also quite efficient in cutting exact 45° angles for moldings up to 3″ wide. But the chopping blade must be kept quite sharp. In narrow and medium size moldings it has an advantage over the miter box and saw in the rapidity, accuracy, and cleanness of cut made in one or two quick motions. Larger, bulkier, or more cumbersome frame moldings, however, may not fit and you will have to return to the "old" miter box.

One can also always turn to the use of a small protractor which can be lined up on the molding directly, marked off with a pencil at a 45° angle so the molding can be cut freehand with a crosscut saw or backsaw. But this method is most open to error and the least professional, although for one or two frames it may save some money. It will be difficult to produce results as professional as the miter box or guillotine will yield.

MAKING YOUR OWN MITER BOX

You can, if you do not plan to make a great number of frames, build your own miter box out of a 2″ × 4″ and two 1″ × 4″ pine planks.

To begin, check the 2″ × 4″ to see if it is square. Use a *T square* to do this. The T square is another important tool when it comes to checking 90° angles (as formed by two 45° mitered edges, for example). Place the T square against the 2″ × 4″, hold the square and wood in line with your eye and a light. Now, drawing the square toward you following the surface of the board, check to be certain there are no buckles or ridges or warping in the wood (which will be evidenced by light leaking through the T square/wood edge).

If there are irregularities, either use another, truer piece of 2″ × 4″ or use a *block plane* to square the wood. (The block plane is an important tool when it comes to correcting minor errors in workmanship or merchandise.) Recheck with the T square. The block plane is not essential, but it is a helpful tool. Taking a sliver of wood off an edge may be all that is needed to correct a bad alignment.

Also use the T square to see that the two 1″ × 4″s are also square. Nail a 1″ × 4″ to each of the two 2″ deep sides of the 2″ × 4″.

As shown in the photographs, set the exact markings for 45° angle cuts across the top edges of the two 1″ × 4″s. The 2″ × 4″ has become the base of the miter box-to-be. Continue this angle marking down the sides of the two planks keeping the lines exactly perpendicular to the face of the 2″ × 4″.

Toward the end of the U-shaped box, also draw markings for a right-angle (90°) groove—this is just a convenience to assure that all straight cuts *are* 90° and not an inappropriate 89° or 91°.

Now cut along the two lines which designate the 45° angle. These cuts must be precise if the miter box is to be of any accuracy and value. Start on the top edge of both boards, carefully checking and rechecking against the T square for accuracy. Saw a little, then recheck. Try to keep the saw (an 11- or 12-point fine crosscut saw is best here) perpendicular to the two planks, using no angle in the sawing. After cutting down to the base 2″ × 4″ face, cut a little more into the 2″ × 4″ along the 45° angle grooves to serve as a sighting line for cutting moldings. Similarly, cut the 90° square line which you marked earlier. Notice that the two 45° angle grooves have been cut so that one points left and the other points right. Obviously, this is because opposite ends of each molding strip must be mitered with one right- and one left-hand 45° angle to butt against the other strips. By cutting the two grooves you need never turn a piece of molding upside down to cut it. Accurate cutting is aided by keeping the molding at all times braced *flat* and flush against the intersecting planes of the 2″ × 4″ face and far 1″ × 4″ wall.

Whenever you need to cut a mitered corner, place the molding on the face of the 2″ × 4″ against the far 1″ × 4″ wall, and line up your penciled-on measurement markings with the sawed groove you made in the 2″ × 4″ face. Then either clamp the molding down or hold it firmly with your left hand. Slide your crosscut saw into the proper 45° angle channel holding it in the same position, and with firm even strokes then cut the molding. But beware! If your homemade miter box produces angles which are not exactly 90° and 45° you might as well scrap it—nothing but these exact angles will suffice.

This homemade miter box uses the crosscut saw, but most commercial miter boxes are made for *backsaws*. This is a saw with a metal "spine" across its top edge which adds a rigidity and accuracy of cut very welcome in framing. Without a spine, a saw may bend or wobble slightly, affecting the cutting angle. If purchasing a backsaw, it should be approximately 18″ to 20″ long, 4″ to 6″ wide, and have about twelve teeth per inch. This length permits the cutting of a mitered edge in a fewer number of strokes, adding to the exactness of the cut.

THE OTHER TOOLS

Other important tools besides the miter box, saw, and other corner-cutting and measuring devices include *angle clamps.* These are used during the joining stage of frame building. The best corners are formed when the mitered edges are exactly 45° angles and when they can be held securely in clamps during gluing and hammering. There is an expensive tool called the Miter Vise and although it does a perfect job, it is unnecessary unless one is going into frame making very seriously. A small corner clamp or two suffice for joining most moldings up to 3″ wide and are essential to anyone planning to make professional-looking frames.

C-Clamps may also be useful, and so can a *bench vise,* although with these tools the trueness of the mitered edges depends on the precision of cutting and less on the assistant clamping devices.

Although not *absolutely* necessary, an *electric hand drill* with a start/stop button in the handle which can be locked "on" is highly recommended. It is used

MAKING A MITER BOX

Sight along the faces of the boards to be used in the miter box using a tri-square, T square, or other tool with a 90° angle to ascertain that the board is not warped. With a block plane, level out all bevels—the 1" × 4"s and the 2" × 4" must be square if the homemade miter box is to work well.

Nail the two 1" × 4"s to the side faces of the 2" × 4" block.

After making sure that the tops of the boards are level (using a level), then, using a right angle, mark off right- and left-hand 45° angles on the top edges. Near one end also mark off for a 90° straight angle cut.

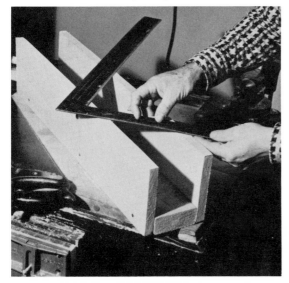

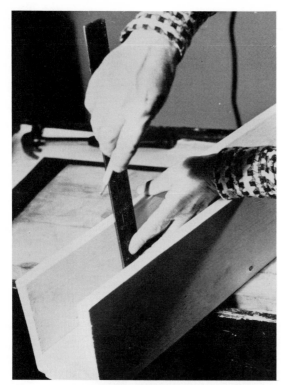

Continue these markings down the sides of the boards to give you a line to follow when cutting the grooves into the miter box.

With an 11 or 12 fine point crosscut saw, cut the grooves. Keep the saw parallel to the 2″ × 4″ base as you cut. Don't let one 1″ × 4″ get farther ahead of the other in the cutting. Cut the right-hand and left-hand grooves as well as the 90° groove. Let the saw ride a little into the face of the 2″ × 4″—this creates a groove which acts as a guide-line along which to align measured moldings.

constantly in the joining of moldings by drilling the path for nails. Drilling a hole slightly smaller than the nail diameter before driving in a nail can help to avoid splitting thin and grainy moldings.

Other essentials for the frame maker are a medium-weight *hammer* (claw variety is fine), a combination *pliers* (or perhaps two pliers, one needle-nosed and one square-nosed), *rulers, nail set,* white all-purpose *glue* (such as Elmer's Glue-All or Sobo), and assorted *finishing nails, brads, screw eyes, braided picture wire,* and *paper* for backing.

A nail set is a pointed metal tool used to sink nails into wood so that the nailheads will not be visible. It is placed on the head of a nail or brad which has been hammered into a frame, and, with a few hammer taps, drives the nail a little below the wood surface. This process is called "countersinking" of nails or brads. Driving the nail below the surface leaves room for wood fillers which hide the nails' presence. Although you may eventually want to obtain a set of nail sets of varying diameters, a 1/16″ nail set is a versatile size to begin with.

Since accuracy is of paramount importance, you *must* have good rulers. For measuring wood, a collapsible wood ruler with a metal edge is best. But a straight yardstick—with a metal edge or made entirely of metal—is absolutely necessary.

While once only rabbit-skin and other inconvenient pastes and glues were recommended for various frame-making processes, plastics technology has brought us *polyvinyl acetate*—that white liquid glue which is strong, fast-drying, water-soluble before hardening, and readily available. You may want to purchase this glue in a squeeze container—or buy a squeeze container separately—since this is a convenient way of dispensing the glue to the narrow surfaces of molding ends and backs.

Along with a variety of finishing nails, brads and *diamond* or *triangle points* are the most common fasteners in this craft. Typically, when bracing a picture into its frame, the frame maker will use ½″ brads (#18) which can be squeezed into the back of the rabbet with pliers. Triangle points may be squeezed in the same way or as with diamond points, must be driven in with a *glazier's gun* against a frame which has been properly braced before the point is shot in. Brads and points are usually spaced at approximate four-inch intervals, wedged in to keep the picture, mats, and/or glass snug against the frame lip.

To seal the back of a picture and frame from dust, *kraft paper* is used. Krafts, which are used for bulk wrappings and paper bags, are available in rolls and sheets. It is usually dampened slightly before being glued to the frame's back. When the paper dries it shrinks taut over the back of the frame.

For hanging, *screw eyes* and braided picture hanging wire are essential. Select the size of screw eye for the size of the molding and the weight of the frame and picture. A screw eye which is too thick will crack the molding while one which is too thin may be torn out by the weight. Braided wire is recommended over single strand because it is much stronger. Once again, the weight of wire should be based on the weight of the frame.

Incidental tools which may be helpful include a *hole punch* or an *awl* (for starting holes), assorted *rollers* (for smoothing out fabrics and paper in matmaking and frame backing), a *brush* for spreading glue, and a *wire cutter* for snipping picture wire and removing nails and brads.

The *glass cutter* is another useful tool. The tool is quite inexpensive and consists of a small rotating wheel which scores a slim channel into the glass— a line along which the glass breaks easily.

Glass Cutting and Application

In framing, glass is usually used for covering surfaces that need special protection: delicate watercolors, pastels, prints and other graphics, fabrics, and some three-dimensional objects that soil easily. Generally, glass should be used to prevent dust from accumulating on lint-prone mats and objects.

Sixteen-ounce *picture glass* is generally advised rather than regular window glass. It has greater optical clarity because it is thinner and is also absolutely free of distortions unless mechanically flawed. Also available is nonglare or "nonreflective" glass. Although this has the advantage of reducing reflections, it also slightly reduces optical clarity, diminishing visibility of fine details and color of some works of art. It is also often very expensive.

Picture glass comes in a variety of sizes from 8″ × 10″ to 18″ × 24″ and 30″ × 40″. The cutting tool is so inexpensive that when it grows dull you may throw it away. To prolong the glass cutter's life, keep the wheel end in kerosene to prevent rusting, and occasionally oil the wheel's axle.

For best results, follow a few important rules when cutting glass: (1) never draw the cutter over the same cut more than once—this dulls the rotating wheel and can shatter the glass; (2) practice your cutting technique on scraps of glass until you can control the tool; (3) when breaking off small pieces of glass use a square-nosed pliers—not your fingers; (4) when cutting, always start with the glass cutter at the edge farthest from you, drawing the tool toward you as you firmly incise—don't be afraid to apply some pressure.

Work on a flat, smooth surface. Begin by measuring the exact size that you want the glass to be—this is usually done by duplicating the measurements of the rabbet size if you are cutting the glass after having made the frame. This size should fall within 1/16″ of the rabbet size, and is generally identical to the mat or mount size as well.

Having marked off the dimensions of the glass with a soft lead pencil or fine crayon, place a metal straightedge (ruler) along the line to be cut. Hold the glass cutter firmly between the index and middle fingers and thumb (as shown). Dip the tip in kerosene and apply even, moderate pressure while drawing the tool across the glass along the metal guide. Move the glass cutter slowly and firmly toward you in a continuous stroke. If you stop in the middle and try to start the cut again it may lead to imperfections in the cut edge. The incision creates a pale white line. A confident, continuous line will make the difference between success and failure.

After scoring the glass, place it at the table's edge. Allow the excess piece to overhang, and keep the scored surface facing up. Firmly grasp the excess glass edge, raise it just slightly, and then snap it sharply on the table edge. With a jolt, the excess glass should crack off neatly along your score line. An alternative method is to place pencils or another slender wooden object at either end under the edge of the glass to be broken. Place these "elevators" just slightly to the "good" side of the white scored line, and tap the glass on the excess side all along the line using the blunt ball end of the glass cutter. It should then snap off along the line.

In the event that both these procedures fail to break off the glass, try turning the glass over (scored line now face down). Gently tap along the length of the cut with the blunt end of the cutter. If this fails too, make another incision on the backside of the glass as you originally did for the other side, and try cracking it as before. But remember, never run the wheel through the same cut line twice.

One further note is on getting the glass clean. Use only water or alcohol for cleaning picture glass. Commercial products or soaps often streak the glass or electrostatically attract lint. You may use some ammonia in the water for very dirty glass. Always clean and dry with a soft cloth, and remember to clean both sides of the glass since dirt and flaws on either side will mar the beauty of the final frame and print.

Having matted and backed your print (see processes in Chapter 2) cut a piece of picture glass by first lining up the glass and measuring the exact size on a piece of flat carpet, heavy cardboard, or Neolite (shoe sole material).

Gripping the glass cutter as shown (between middle and index fingers with index finger on top and bracing by thumb) start your cut at the point farthest from you. Use a metal ruler to guide the cutting. Apply some pressure to make a groove in the glass, and execute it with one continuous, even stroke.

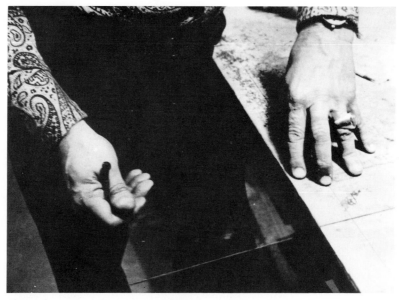

Bring the scored line to the table edge and crack off the excess—it should snap off along the line. If not, turn the glass over and tap along the line with the blunt ball end of the glass cutter.

Cutting and Joining the Molding

Making a simple, basic frame is technically quite easy. This basic process is the single most important concept in frame making; and its mastery will allow you to create the most involved combinations of frames. First measure the four molding strips, remembering to leave the necessary excess at each end of the moldings for miter cuts. (Add on *twice* the *width* of the molding strip to each piece plus an inch or two extra for sawing. For example, if using a 2″ wide molding strip to frame a painting which is 18″ long, you need to measure and cut a piece of molding 18″ (the rabbet size) plus two times 2″, or 18″ + 4″ + (extra length for error) 1″ = 23″.

Cut the molding at a right angle, 90°, first. Then set your miter box and backsaw or your chopper for all right-hand 45° cuts. (We choose to do all right-hand cuts first simply as a matter of convenience.) Execute those cuts.

A time-saver and accuracy aid is to measure the length of one molding strip from another strip already cut. This saves the remeasuring from the original picture, and also assures that opposite sides of the final frame will be identical (and therefore will be square when joined). Use a *stop block* when using a miter box. A stop block is simply a piece of wood clamped onto the molding strip being cut. The block has a 45° mitered end already which, while marking the proper cutting line for a piece of molding, also helps guide the saw to a perfect cut. It is simply a device for stopping the molding from being cut longer than its match. Of course using a stop block or even measuring one molding strip from another implies two things: (1) you originally measured correctly from the picture to the first molding strips and (2) the picture you are framing is a perfect rectangle. It is always wise to confirm both of these points before cutting.

MAKING THE BASIC FRAME
Measure the exact lengths of molding needed. To each measured length add two times the width of the molding, plus $\frac{1}{16}''$ at each end for saw error.

First cut the lengths of molding with a straight 90° angle.

Miter the right and left ends. Shown here is the hand guillotine (chopper) which with a swift lever action slices perfect 45° angles into molding bars.

Clamping the longer strip of molding in a table vise or in an angle clamp, apply glue to the mitered end. Join the proper ends together into a perfect (smooth, flush) corner. Do this for the entire frame. You may choose to do the next three steps in the process for each glued corner before proceeding to glue the subsequent three corners.

After the glue has dried, leave the frame in the vise or clamps, drill nail holes with an electric drill and a drill bit which is slightly thinner than the nails will be. For a frame this thin, two nails per joint is sufficient.

Drive in the brads.

The brads or nails should enter the joint from both sides in medium and larger frames.

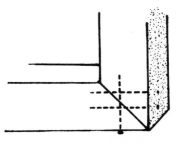

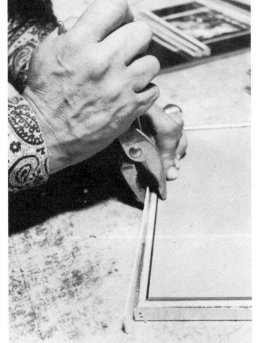

Countersink the brads slightly below the surface of the frame using a nail set. Later these holes will be filled in with a wood filler of the appropriate color for the finish.

Finishing could be the next process, but the molding of this frame had already been gold leafed (see Chapter 4 on finishes). If you need to finish the wood, at this point add the finishes before proceeding. Place clean glass, mat, print, and backing face down in the frame. Squeeze brads into the back of the rabbet three to four inches apart so that the picture and assembly are held firmly against the lip of the frame front. Use a strip of waste wood to protect the outer finished surface of the frame from pliers marks. (Or cover the outer plier with adhesive felt.)

With a knife, press filler into all nail holes. A metallic waxlike material is used on this gold leaf. Some trade names are Treasure Gold and Rub'n Buff.

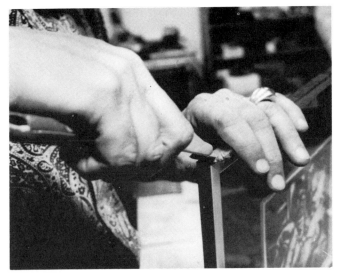

Having cut the four strips at one end with a right-hand 45° angle, now recheck the lengths against the painting's edge according to rabbet size, and cut all the left-hand 45° angles. When cutting, saw barely to the outside of your pencil marks. This is the *saving line,* and cutting outside of your marks should guarantee that no pieces of molding are cut too short.

As you proceed, also recheck the miter box or chopper to be certain that it is producing exact 45° angles. Check this by butting right- and left-hand 45° angled ends together, and checking the corner for skewness with a T square or right angle. Readjust the saw or chopper if it is off angle.

If you are using a regular workbench vise to join pieces, it is a good practice to put the longer piece of molding in the vise with the mitered edge slightly above the jaws. Before gluing always check to be certain you are not joining the wrong corners—i.e. butting two parallels together. If using angle clamps, put the two strips in the clamps. Align them so that they butt perfectly, then remove one from the clamp. Leave the other one firmly in place.

Apply your all-purpose white glue to the mitered edge. Use enough to form a firm bond, but not so much that it is squeezed out of the joint. Spread the glue evenly with a finger, stick, or brush; replace the strip in the clamp and again match it exactly with its corner mate. Allow the glued corner to dry. Follow the same procedure for the other pair of strips that form the opposite corner. Then glue the pairs of molding strips together to complete the frame. You may find it more effective to use two angle clamps at this step and glue opposite corners simultaneously.

Either before or after the gluing step you should plan to drill nail holes with an electric drill. With larger moldings you should probably drill your two or three holes in each corner *before* gluing. But in smaller, less hard-to-manage frames, it doesn't really matter whether you drill before or after. When drilling (and of course nailing, too) after gluing, be certain that the glue has dried. Leave the joints in the clamps while you drill and hammer.

Holes drilled with a drill bit slightly thinner than the nails will both guide the nails and prevent the molding from splitting. Hammer in all nails (finishing nail size should be determined according to the width of the molding, i.e., 1½″ molding requires fourpenny finishing nails while a narrow ½″ molding needs only #17 or #18 wire brads of ¾″ to 1″ length). Now use a nail set to sink the nails slightly beneath the frame's surface. The holes can later be filled in with the appropriate color filler (see Chapter 4 on finishing).

If you have been working with a builder's molding without a rabbet, at this point you will want to add on the ½″ × ¾″ rabbet rectangle to the back of the frame (as described earlier in the chapter). Otherwise you are ready to finish the frame. But before finishing, check to see how well the picture fits. In fact, you may want to check this before nailing the frame together. You should always check as best you can after each step. Glass, mat, mount, and/or picture should slide easily into the rabbet. There should be a slight slack; no part should be forced into the rabbet. When viewed from the front, however, you should not be able to see the edge of a mat because the frame was either too long or too wide.

If, on trial fitting, the picture sits well in the frame and looks good, then add the surface finishes. So much of what the final product looks like depends upon finishing, as seen in Chapter 4. After finishing, place the frame face down on a clean working area, and place the mats, mounts, picture, and glass in proper sequence face down in the frame. You will notice that the rabbet usually projects higher than the back of the mount or picture backing, except in some instances with stretched canvases. In most cases, therefore, to fix the picture firmly in the frame, squeeze ½″ wire brads into the back of the rabbet with a pair of pliers. A piece of scrap wood held against the outer finished edge of the frame molding will guarantee that no marks from the pliers will mar the finish. Flannel tape (used in shoes or on feet) wrapped around the outer jaw of the pliers will also protect the frame. Set the brads several inches apart (depending on the size and weight of the material being enclosed) and squeeze them in so that the picture is wedged firmly against the lip of the frame. You may also use diamond points shot from a glazier's gun to keep the picture in its frame. If you choose this method, brace the frame against a wooden block so that the shock of the shots does not jolt the frame and break the glass.

If you are framing a canvas that was done on stretcher bars, you may find that (unless the molding has been given an especially deep rabbet made especially for stretched canvas pictures) the stretcher will protrude past the depth of the rabbet. To affix the frame and picture in this case you may either drive long finishing nails (sixpenny nails, for example) through the stretcher bars and into the back of the frame at an angle, or else screw on S-shaped clamps which are available at hardware stores. Using the clamps permits the easy removal of the painting from the frame at a later date. But since you are making the frame, buy molding that is made to accommodate the depth of the canvas stretcher, if you can (or add a deep enough rabbet to builder's molding).

Before finally bracing the picture with brads and points, however, lift the frame and check to be certain that the glass is clean and that mats and work of art are clear of lint, debris (called "crabs"), and imperfections. Dark, especially black, mats are particularly difficult to keep free of crabs. To remove lint you may want to use wide masking tape and, with the sticky face out, form a circle that fits around your fist. Roll this sticky fist over the mat until the tape has picked up all crabs and dust. Then proceed to affix the picture in the frame as described above.

The Final Touches

To keep dust out of the finished frame, seal the back with brown kraft paper. With the frame still face down on the work area, with glass, mat, mounts, and backing inside, cut a piece of brown kraft paper (this is the normal wrapping paper) to a size slightly larger than the entire back of the frame. Apply the white glue around the perimeter of the frame's back. Dampen (but don't soak) the kraft paper with a sponge and lay it over the entire back of the frame so that it conforms to the frame's shape. If you use a heavy weight paper, dampening may be unnecessary. With fingers and, if you like, a small wallpapering roller, smooth the paper over the glued areas until it adheres to the frame. The paper will be quite taut when it dries. With a single-edge safety razor blade or X-acto knife, trim off the excess paper ¼″ in from the outside edge of the frame back.

Now all you need are a few screw eyes through which to string braided picture-hanging wire. For most pictures and their frames, two eyes should suffice. Choose an appropriate screw eye size for the weight and width of the frame and picture. The eyes should be screwed no more than a third of the way down from the top edge of the frame. Otherwise the picture will noticeably tilt downward from the top. Measure this ⅓ distance so that the screw eyes are even with each other. To start the screws, use an awl or hole punch.

To complete the framing job, cut a piece of Kraft (brown wrapping) paper into the approximate size of the entire frame back. Apply white glue to the back edge of the frame. Lay the paper on top and smooth it down until it adheres. Even pressure of a wallpaper roller can help in adhering it.

Trim the excess paper just shy of the edge, on the inside of the frame back, guiding the razor blade with a ruler or straightedge.

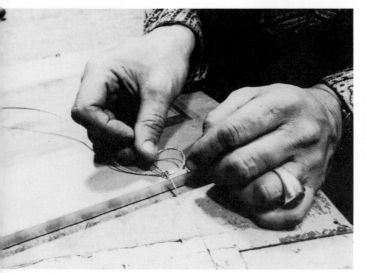

Insert screw eyes into the molding approximately one-third of the way down from the top edge. Thread braided picture hanging wire through the eyes to form a circle and wrap the wire around itself tightly.

Leave enough slack in the wire so that the picture wire can reach the wall hook, and yet not allow the frame to tip downward when hanging. Notice that the credits for the print are taped to the kraft paper backing.

A Family Group by the Chinese artist Liu Te Hua (*upper right*) and *Arch Criminal of August 13th Incident* by Hsu Yun Pao (*lower left*) were both framed as described, using narrow flat gold molding. The mats are black mount board and the old woodblock prints from China are both set on countermounts of mat gold to add accent and to repeat the color of the frame.

In very large paintings, you will want to distribute the weight better among *four* screw eyes placed as shown in the diagram. Notice that the exact location of the lower eyes is not as important as their symmetry in relation to the picture's midpoint.

The braided wire (which should be doubled over and rebraided for very heavy frames) should be looped through the eyes twice and then wrapped around itself for three or four inches at each end. See that no wire is left dragging. The wire should *not* be absolutely taut between the eyes—there should be just enough slack so that, while not showing above the top of the frame, there is enough to permit the wire to reach the hook or nail in the wall.

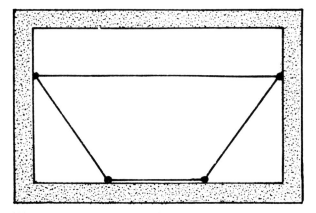

When planning to hang a larger frame, it is wise to insert more than two screw eyes. Support the weight of the frame by setting in four eyes and stringing the braided wire as shown.

With a little hardware, wood, and imagination, many alternative ways of hanging objects (or even standing them up) can be devised.

Sheets of stick-on cork or rubber may be tacked on to the back of frames or to the back inside corners to keep wood finishes from marring the wall, and to permit dust to fall behind the picture and not just settle on or around it. Shown here is a round frame, sporting a cork backing.

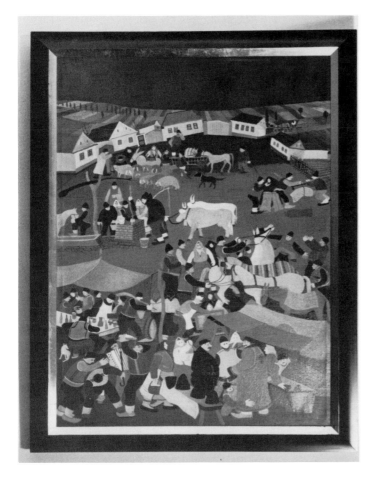

A primitive oil painting by Martin Jonas (1962) is highlighted by a simple molding finished in black and gold leaf on the bevel.

Clouds (1967) by Guyanan artist Phillip Moore is framed using simple butt joints with ¼″ × 2½″ wood strips finished with gold leaf. The exposed inside surface of the frame is painted in flat black. This is perhaps one of the simplest, neatest framing techniques, requiring not even a miter box.

Combining Frame Moldings

After mastering the basic techniques involved in making a one-molding frame, you can easily adapt these skills to inventing combination frames using two or more moldings.

There are advantages to assembling various moldings. For one thing, it permits more variety of direction; it can enlarge a frame into greater widths where more massive proportions are desirable; and it can project a piece farther away from the wall when illusion of depth is desirable. Another plus is that more subtle transitions are possible when several shapes are combined than are usually embodied in a single molding shape. Also, single wide moldings have a greater tendency to warp than an aggregate of narrower forms. Greater variety in size, shape, texture, and profile is possible by combining shapes in different ways. In a combination of moldings, the one nearest the picture may be a liner.

The Liner

One of the most attractive and commonly used frame combinations employs an inside molding covered with fabric—this type of additional frame is called a *liner*. Liners are generally used to separate canvases from what may otherwise be an abrupt transition of frame to picture. Fabric is attached to the molding in the same manner as it is attached in matmaking (see Chapter 2). This molding is cut and joined in the same way as with the basic frame described above, except that you need not countersink nails since all but the face of the liner is hidden by the outer frame.

MAKING A LINER

After the fabric has been glued to the molding to make a liner, measure the liner just as you would a simple frame.

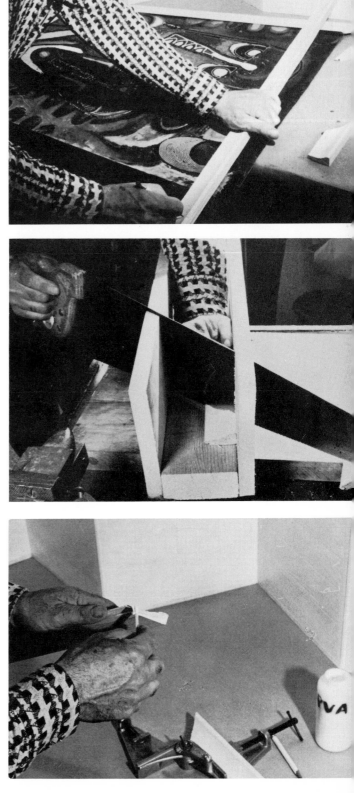

With the liner flush against the back of the miter box, cut the right-hand 45° angle. Recheck measures and cut the left-hand angle as well.

Using an angle clamp, first take the two mitered pieces to be joined and set them in the clamps so that you can check the perfection of your cut. Take one of the two out of the clamp and apply PVA white glue over the entire miter edge. Replace it in the clamp so that the two strips match flush. Let the joint dry. Repeat this for the other liner joints until the liner part of the frame is complete.

There are units on the market today that will clamp an entire frame around its picture to aid in the gluing, drilling, and nailing process. Shown here, for example, is the Frame-Up! by Blank-It Corporation. It can be a helpful brace to the busy framer.

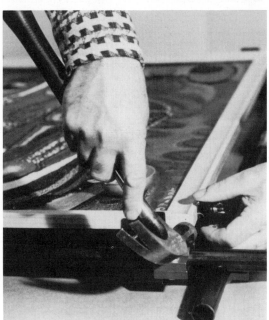

After drilling holes, drive the nails into the liner.

Nail from both sides of the joint.

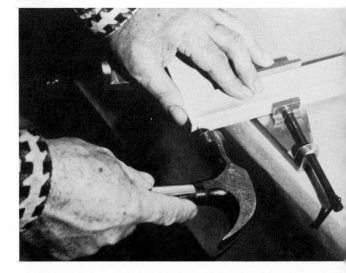

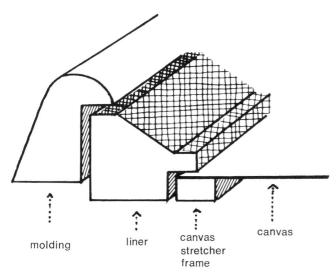

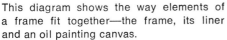

molding   liner   canvas stretcher frame   canvas

This diagram shows the way elements of a frame fit together—the frame, its liner and an oil painting canvas.

After constructing the outer frame to fit around the liner following the procedure for the basic frame, touch up any rough spots in the finish of the outer molding, such as filling in chipped paint at corners with the appropriate color of filler and/or acrylic paint. Nail the outer frame to the inner lining with the same type of brads used for corners and apply finishing touches where necessary.

Having squeezed in brads or shot in points with a glazier's gun to hold the picture firmly in the liner-frame, apply glue to the edge of the frame back.

Lay kraft paper across the back. Press the paper onto the glued edge until it adheres. Cut off excess paper.

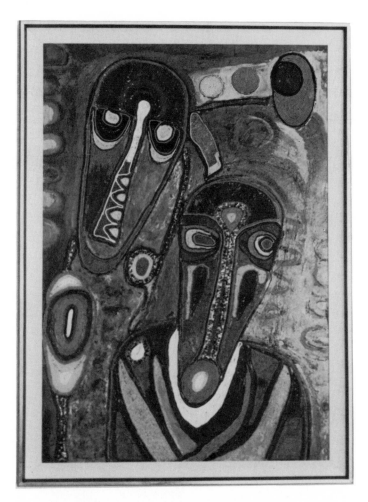

Dancers by Buraimoh, a Nigerian artist, created with oils and beads on plywood. It is framed with a linen liner; its outer frame finished in gold leaf tries to capture some of the colorful liveliness of the beadwork. Perhaps this frame would have been more successful with a wider liner and a bolder frame.

A primitive by Ivan Generalic, oil painting on glass, was set in this combination of liner and narrow round molding. A thin strip of gold leaf trims and accentuates the inside edge of the linen liner.

A similar frame, using a liner without a gold accent, describes this picture differently. This painting, on glass, is by Stephan Večenaj of Yugoslavia.

A corner of a liner showing a beautiful job of joining.

In making the liner frame, treat the liner measurements according to rabbet size. (Again, make the rabbet size for the liner slightly larger than the canvas being fitted inside.) The uncovered frame which will go on the outside of the liner must be made large enough to accommodate the added width of the liner. To avoid mistakes in this process, you may want to make the liner frame first and measure the dimensions of that frame before proceeding to make the outer frame which must fit exactly over it. Attach the finished liner and frame with nails or brads driven in from the side and back.

Just as you may use a liner to add variety, style, and transition to a frame, you may use any other combination of moldings—with or without fabrics, of the same finish, or different finishes. As shown in the diagrammed combinations of "molding profiles," the way in which you "stack" frames adds even more dimension.

The natural wood finish of this frame complements the texture found in this collage by Jane Bearman. A liner of linen edged with gold is used as a transition from picture to frame.

A translucent tissue paper collage by V. Osterland is framed with a combination of two moldings. The inner molding is of white wood. The inward bevel of the molding combination helps to affirm the sense of perspective found in this seascape.

A spectrum of frame moldings (including liners at right). All of these moldings can be combined . . .

. . . into many different combinations.

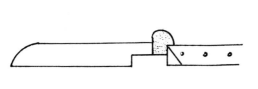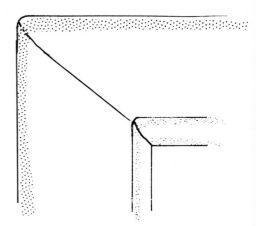

This profile of a combination frame and a projection of a corner is an example of using a broad flat molding curved at the outer edge, with a half-round inner molding which makes the transition to the canvas. This is the same combination design shown in Chapter 1 for "Jack." Curved mitered joints can be made by sanding the corners after gluing and nailing, but before finishing.

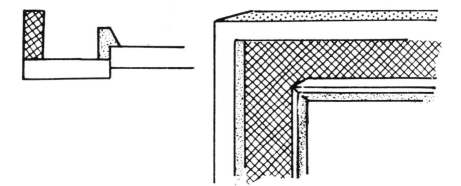

A bevel reverse molding (inside) combined with flat wood strips becoming a fabric-covered liner, and an outer strip of flat wood, forms a handsome "moat" around the picture.

Cove builder's molding nailed onto a simple bevel frame molding adds an inward slant to the frame.

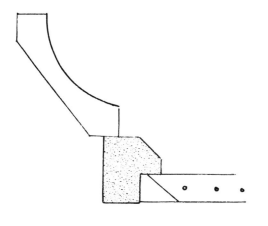

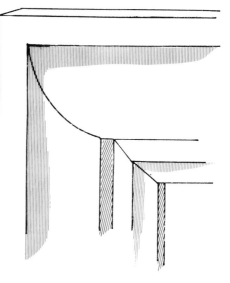

A photomontage by Thelma R. Newman takes on a special import when framed in a combination frame. Notice the projecting inner molding is painted on the inner face with black to sharply define and restate the photomontage's blacks. While most photographs look best with a white mat, a gray mat was used here. If white had been used, the white in the photomontage would have been indistinguishable from the white mat.

Combining clamshell molding with beveled high-back molding discreetly sets off the black mat surrounding this linoleum block print (in red) on fabric (beige).

Making a Shadow Box

There are two main types of shadow boxes: one that uses the *double frame* technique, and another called the *lined box* that calls for only one molding.

The lined box type consists of extradeep rabbet—deep enough to accommodate glass and the three-dimensional object. The glass is kept flush against the lip of the frame by using spacers (also called "fillets"). These fillets may either be made of appropriately finished wood strips or of extrathick mat board which is covered with the same fabric or pattern as is used on the mount. The mat board is cut in strips wide enough to brace the backing and glass apart. It is glued in place to the inside of the rabbet. Either fillet of mat or wood strip forms a vertical wall wide enough to support glass in front of, and not leaning on or touching, the object.

The double frame technique is identical to putting a liner inside the outer frame, except that a sheet of picture glass is put in between the outer molding and the inner one before nailing the two moldings together.

The object itself—be it collage, relief, or some three-dimensional form—is attached to its mounting board either by sewing it with an invisible nylon thread, fishing line, or wire or by gluing. The best shadow boxes are those which are discreet about how the objects have been fastened onto the mount. Also best are those boxes which most appropriately relate size of frame, size of mat, and depth of box to one another.

SHADOW BOXES

There are more than a few ways of creating a shadow box. The double-frame technique at top wedges the glass between moldings, the inner molding becoming a liner-fillet. The middle example (which is made in the following photo sequence) supports the glass, using diamond or triangle points which are shot into the inner frame with a glazier's gun and then sealed with Epoxy glue. The bottom example requires only one frame molding and a wood or thin mat board strip called a fillet. The fillet supports the glass above the mount and object.

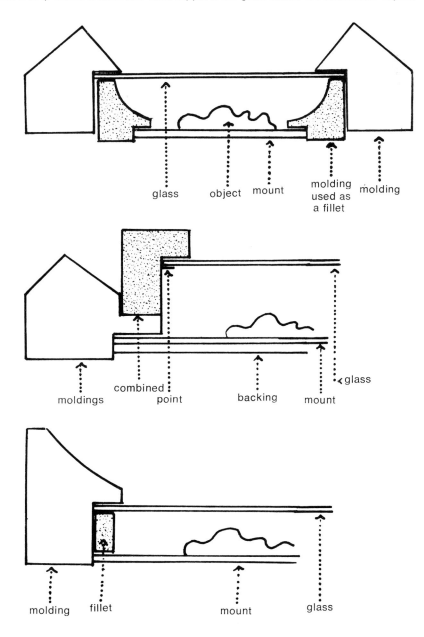

glass object mount molding used as a fillet molding

moldings combined point backing mount glass

molding fillet mount glass

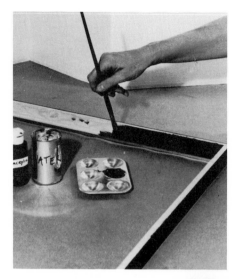

In planning a shadow box, remember that in some cases (depending upon the design) the inside of one molding may be seen. Here the inside of the molding is being painted with an acrylic paint (black) thinned with water.

To fill in any gaps in mitered edges and to fill in the holes left by countersinking nails, mix acrylic paint with modeling paste. This filler mixture can be combined with any color. If you are finishing wood, save a bit of the color for coloring the filler.

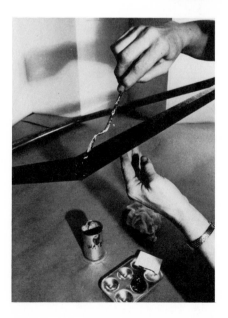

Press the mixture into holes with a knife or spatula.

After completing the inside and outside frames, nail them together. If you are making the double frame type of shadow box with a fillet, then remember to insert the glass between moldings before carefully nailing the two together. Do drill holes for nails first to minimize impact.

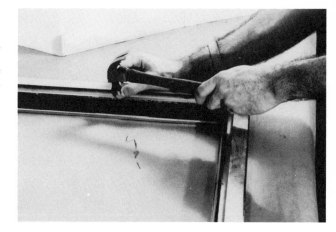

In this shadow box, we chose to mount the objects on velvet-covered plywood. Cut the velvet several inches larger than the plywood board and then staple or tack it on the back.

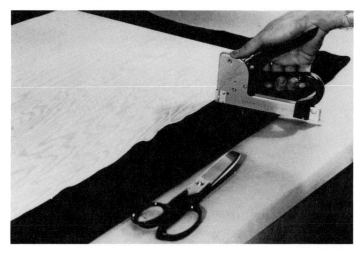

At the corners, cut away the excess overlapping velvet . . .

. . . and staple the velvet flat at the corners.

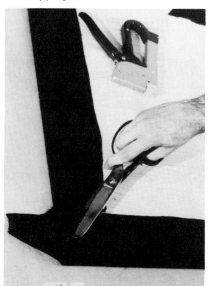

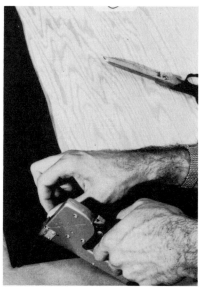

The Ecuadorian bread figure and the Mexican beaded collar are sewed onto the velvet backing with polyester thread, or nylon monofilament (fishing line).

All lint is removed from the back velvet (which incidently is a particular problem to keep clear of lint) by curling masking tape into a loop with sticky side out.

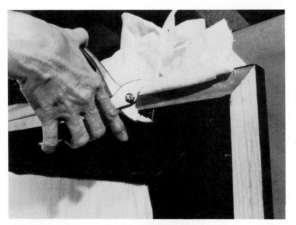

After inserting glass and mount, squeeze brads into the back of the rabbet. Again, be careful to keep plier marks from scarring the outside finish.

Glue kraft paper to the back of the shadow box to keep dust out. Then with a hole punch or an awl, tap holes one-third of the way down from the top into which screw eyes can be set.

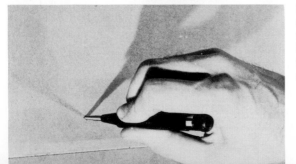

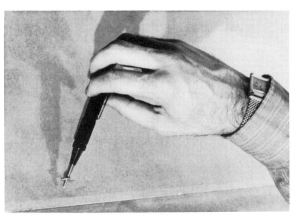

To get the screw eyes to go in easily all the way, use the tip of the awl as a lever.

The completed shadow box using two frames with glass held in place with points stabilized with Epoxy.

An example of a shadow box preserving paper tole, a composition of three-dimensional paper flowers. The flowers are set on a silk moire countermount, fronted with gold-edged velvet liner, all contained in a gold leaf molding.

Passe-Partout

One other framing technique which should be mentioned is passe-partout, a simple, direct way of temporarily and inexpensively preserving and displaying prints, photographs, drawings, engravings, watercolors. All it requires is glass (or acrylic), a mat, backing, hangers, and plastic cloth or adhesive tape to bind the edges.

Simply cut the glass or acrylic, mat, and backing as described earlier. Assemble all parts, taking special care that the glass is clean. Attach "passe-partout rings" (which are small ring hangers attached to flaps) by pushing the rings through slits made in the backing. Glue and tape down the flaps, or create hangers out of tape. After lining up the backing with the glass and mat, cut a strip of tape about one inch longer than the edge to be taped together. Lay the tape in a straight line along the front of the glass with ¼″ overlap onto the front. Use a metal straightedge to guide the tape in an even line. Make certain there are no wrinkles in the tape as you smooth it out. Now, being careful to keep the glass, mat, and backing lined up and square along the edges, fold the tape back and stick it to the rear of the backing. A cross-section of the tape should look like a U. Trim off excess tape at the ends and repeat this end-sealing process for the opposite edge. Corners can also be cut into a miter shape. Seal all four sides. Slip braided wire through the rings and hang the completed frame. That's all there is to it.

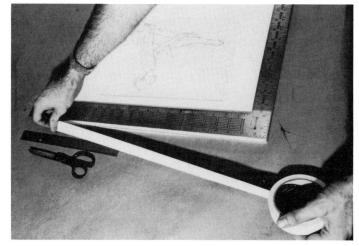

PASSE-PARTOUT

After setting the print in a mat and sandwiching it between glass (or acrylic) and backing, tape the edges with a plastic tape. Let the tape overlap on the front by about one-fourth inch. Keep this tape line straight by setting your metal ruler down as a guide.

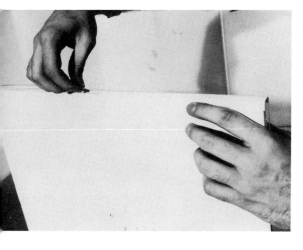

Bring the tape around to the back side of the passe-partout frame. Repeat this sealing on the other three sides. The tape forms a "U" channel all around the mount, backing, and glass, creating a simple, but effective and inexpensive, frame.

Nude print from an etching in acrylic by Jane Bearman. The finished passe-partout is a neat, light, inexpensive framing method. While picture glass may be used, lightweight acrylic (which has comparable optical clarity) is used here. Tape hangers are used on the back.

FINISHING
AND
REFINISHING

Although there are frames made of ceramic, leather, metal, paper, and plastic, as illustrated farther on, the focus here is on wood—how to treat unfinished wood, as well as how to revitalize old frames. Both offer enormous possibilities. The basic techniques described here can be expanded upon and combined into more personal finishes, uniquely your own. The mechanics of putting together a frame, once mastered, are not nearly so interesting as combining mats, liners with frames, and designing finishes to suit a particular work of art. As indicated earlier in this book, there is no one possibility, nor are there any hard-and-fast rules that govern designs of frames and their finishes. The potential is open-ended, with much room for creativity. One of the most exciting experiences is taking an old beat-up frame that is the right size for your art work and making something "superb" out of it.

Finishes used to take a great deal of time because each coat of paint and varnish would take a day to dry. It was very time consuming. Now with new plastic finishes—vinyl, urethane, acrylic and acrylic gesso, and modeling paste—mostly water-soluble—laborious work is gone and the fun is left.

Kinds of Wood Frames

Frames usually are made of soft wood, such as pine. There are solid oak, birch, beech, walnut, wormy chestnut, spruce, cherry, maple, and mahogany moldings available as well as more exotic woods. Builder's moldings, though, are most commonly pine, birch, or oak. Soft woods such as pine have an unimportant grain, texture, color, or surface. These lend themselves to gesso, gold

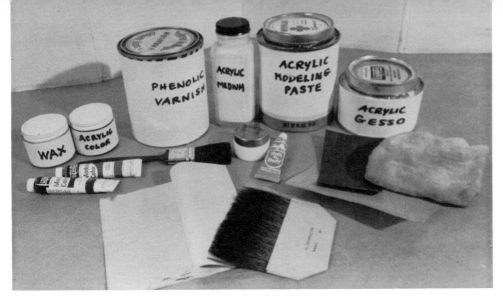

These are basic materials for finishing and refinishing frames. In the foreground are gold leaf and its brush. On the right is tack cloth; next to it are sandpapers. The rest are various kinds of colors, bases, and varnishes.

Starting with a basic oak frame that has a rough grain, an antique effect can be achieved by using a toothbrush to roughly apply assorted neutral acrylic colors.

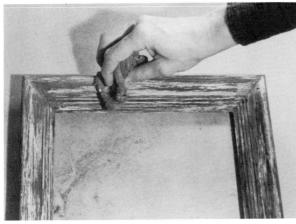

Excess can be sanded away with a fine steel wool. Then tack cloth is used to dust away steel grit before another application of color is made.

The completed frame with grays and browns to further define its grain.

leafing, lacquer, paint, and other opaque finishes. Woods with beautiful grain and color such as walnut and cherry should be oiled or varnished to bring out their natural colors and textures.

One also can use beat-up wood such as barn siding, and distressed wood that has seen weathering and wear. But these have a limited potential in relatively few applications. Although there are many novelty effects possible that are handsome for their own sake, they can distract the eye from what is being framed. (The same is true of the gingerbread monstrosities of yesteryear.) Try not to be carried away by the surprise of an effect, but rather, always ask, "What does this finish do for what is being framed? Does it complement or detract?"

Basic Colors and Effects

To the cook who is a master of sauces, there are basic meat and fish stocks that, once made, are stored for a week or two and employed for many uses. And to the framer, there are basic materials that underlie most possibilities. It is a good idea to mix acrylic color into neutral gray-beige, one batch on the warm side, the other on the cool side, and to store these in jars for future use. These are often called patina. They serve the purposes of providing a finish on raw wood and gesso and antiquing over other colors as well as gilded frames. For the cooler tone, start with white acrylic, and add a touch each of raw umber and ochre. And for a warm tone on the pink side, start with white, and add ochre and a touch of alizarin crimson. These are light neutrals. It is possible to create patinas that are darker in tone by starting with a cool gray as a base for the cool patina, and with umber as a base for warmer effects.

Oil, another basic, most often linseed oil, is rubbed into wood to bring out natural color and texture as well as to preserve it. Several applications are needed at first, and then every six to twelve months. A lemon and crude oil mixture can also be used.

Metallic effects can be created by waxlike paste colors that are rubbed on and act as patinas or accents of color, or by using synthetic or natural gold or silver leaf.

Varnishes of various kinds can also be used. Some come pigmented, others are applied over staining, and when applied in many coats and sanded, can approach a beautiful furniture finish. Whenever possible, these varnish finishes should be used while the molding is in one piece to avoid difficulties in sanding corners.

Then, of course, there is basic black lacquer or black acrylic which is used for graphics of various kinds and as accents in combination with other finishes when two or more moldings are combined.

Basic Texture Effects

Texturing effects can be achieved by a wide variety of techniques: by rubbing patina into coarse-grained wood such as oak, chestnut, spruce; by using acrylic modeling paste and molding or combing textures into it; by burning it with a propane torch; or by physically mutilating it with rasps, files, gouges, chains, and other wood-torturing tools.

Whatever the style of texturing, it needs some further finishing with patinas or a final coat of wax.

One kind of texturing effect that can be very successful is to cover the surface of the wood with another material, such as cork, linen, burlap, or even velvet.

Finishing Raw Wood—A New Approach

Until recently (vestiges of the practice still hang on), to finish wood, the ceremony required an elaborate array of materials such as casein, hide glue, gelatin, copal varnish, pigments and powders, gum resins, shellac, Japan size, and the applicable solvents. Application took skills approaching alchemy and much time and labor. With the miracle of matte and glossy acrylic emulsions, acrylic paints and acrylic gesso and modeling paste, almost all these materials are obsolete. Effects are the same with much less time and labor; and best of all, with a minimum of cleanup—plain water is all that is needed. This does not mean that acrylic, once dry, is water soluble. It is, in fact, *water insoluble* when dry and does not require any treatment if you should want to apply varnishes over it. Therefore, instead of sealers and primers for raw wood, all you need is acrylic emulsion (sometimes called polymer emulsion) to seal and prime raw wood. To stain wood, a water-diluted pigmented acrylic paint will do the job. The patina is acrylic, too. And to texture wood, modeling paste can be manipulated with a spatula, textured with tools such as a comb and then finished with acrylic gesso. When gold-leafing, acrylic gesso forms a smooth base, and acrylic emulsion acts as the adhesive as well as the final protecting finish, if desired.

BASIC PREPARATION OF SURFACE

Fill all cracks and nail holes with acrylic modeling paste or any other filler such as a vinyl, using a flexible spatula tool such as a palette knife or tongue depressor. When dry, filled-in surfaces should be sanded wet or dry with 220 grit wet-or-dry paper.

Then, lightly abrade the entire surface of the frame or molding, creating a "tooth" for other finishes. Sand with 100 grit dry garnet paper following the grain of the wood.

Dust the entire piece with tack cloth, a resinous waxy cloth that lifts away dust specks. Now the piece is ready to receive an oil, gesso, acrylic emulsion, or modeling paste finish. When acrylic is used for each step, no other preparation is necessary. Specific treatment, as for gold leafing, spattering, or antiquing, is described in step-by-step photos in this chapter and throughout the book.

GOLD LEAFING
Pine wood strips are sanded smooth with #160 dry sandpaper.

Dust is removed with a tack cloth.

Three coats of acrylic gesso are applied; after the second coat #400 wet or dry sandpaper is used to smooth the surface.

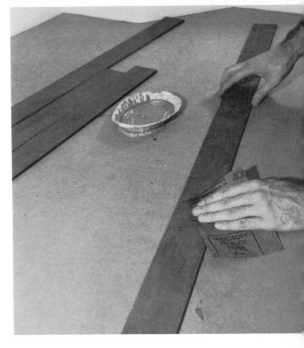

Dark red acrylic is painted over the gesso. This is optional. Later, for antiquing, some red showing through creates a complementing texture. Then the paint is sanded smooth with #400 wet or dry sandpaper.

The other side is painted with black acrylic and then spray-coated with several coats of acrylic matte finishing.

Immediately before applying gold leaf, a coating of acrylic (polymer) medium is added.

Using a flat knife, a measured amount of gold is cut from its sheet.

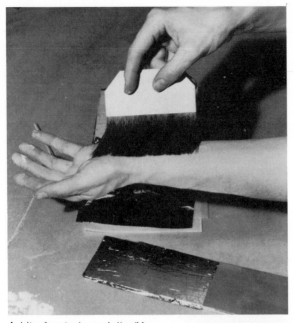

A bit of petroleum jelly (Vaseline) is rubbed on the wrist, and then a gold-leafer's brush is gently brushed across the wrist . . .

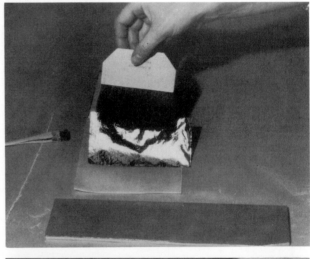

. . . immediately the measured piece of gold leaf is lifted on the brush and . . .

. . . gently placed on the wet acrylic-coated wood.

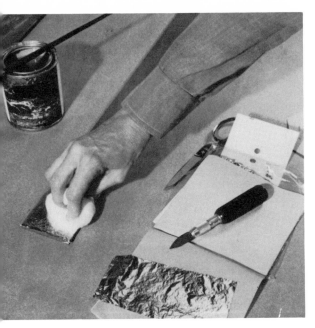

A puff of cotton is used to gently tampen the gold leaf, or . . .

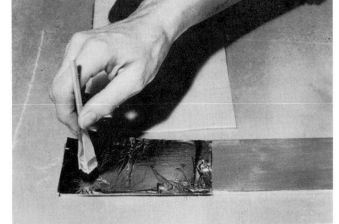

. . . a Japanese tampening brush that has soft bristles can do the job as well.

After all pieces are covered, varnish can be applied as a protective coat. Gold leafing is not easy. It takes much practice to succeed. If your leaf should tear, patching is possible on those breaks that require it, and the effect can even be handsome.

To create an antique effect, some leaf can be rubbed away with alcohol, revealing the red underneath.

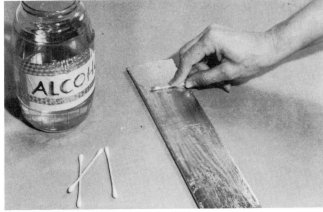

Raw umber and other "antiquing" color then can be used to create an antique effect.

Spattering is accomplished by using a tooth-brush charged with paint (such as umber). A tongue-depressor rubbed across it will send specks flying onto the surface.

Another texturing effect over gold leaf requires blocking off areas with acrylic (for one effect) or varnish (for a different effect).

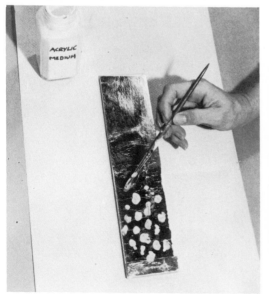

A mixture of 5 or 10 percent sodium sulfide in water will darken areas not protected with varnish. It can be applied with cotton, or . . .

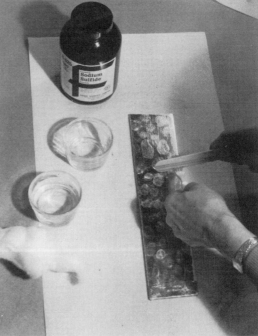

. . . by spattering it with a brush, or . . .

. . . with a toothbrush.

APPLICATION OF GESSO, PAINT, VARNISH

Gesso is usually applied with a brush. Most brands are about as viscous as ketchup. If thinner applications are desired, place some gesso in a small container. To this you may add a small amount of water; stir well until the necessary thickness is achieved.

Paint is applied with a brush. If acrylic paint comes from a tube, squeeze some into a dish or tin and dilute with water if necessary. Dip the brush bristles halfway into the paint, press the excess off on the side of the tin, and holding the brush well up on the handle, apply paint with long, even strokes, following the wood's grain, if possible. Repeat, stroking the paint, with light strokes. This levels the paint and smooths out irregularities, producing a surface with very little unevenness. Check for runs, drips, and sags by smoothing or absorbing excess with a dry brush.

If second and third coats are necessary, allow each coat to dry, lightly sand away any unevenness (if it is undesirable), dust away grit with tack cloth, and brush on the next coat. For very fine smooth surfaces use #000 or #0000 steel wool.

Varnishes should be crystal clear, strong, and elastic. They come in gloss or matte surfaces. Matte varnish contains some wax, pulverized mica, and talc to reduce its luster. Polymer varnishes are diluted with several different diluents. It is important to read directions on the can and follow them because some varnishes should not be stirred, others should, and some require the addition of some distilled turpentine to prevent a skin from forming and to preserve it for future applications. Some varnishes, such as Deft, dry in minutes, others in hours, and still others take days. When varnishing, charge your brush with varnish; press excess off on the inside of the can. Start your strokes in the *middle* of the surface and move to one edge. The following stroke starts in the middle again and carries the varnish to the opposite edge. Continue stroking the brush across the entire surface to the edge until the brush load diminishes before reloading your brush. The first application should be with the grain, but other strokes can follow, across the grain and then again with the grain, using the lightest touch possible. Each stroke should be as delicate as possible without skipping any surface area.

Varnish can be rubbed down with 500 or 600 wet-or-dry (silicon carbide) paper and a sudsy solution of nondetergent soap and water after two coats. After each sanding, remove grit with tack cloth before proceeding to the next coat.

A Summary of Raw Wood Frame Finishes

Numbers indicate sequence of steps

Material	Coarse-grained oak, chestnut, spruce, or pine	Wormy Chestnut	Soft woods	Texturing and Finishing	Medium grained, natural effects
acrylic gesso			1. Coat with 3 coats of gesso; sand level after 2nd and 3rd coats.	1. Brush a light coat of gesso over entire surface. Repeat step after doing "2."	
acrylic modeling paste				2. Comb, mottle, or manipulate with a spatula a thick layer of modeling paste.	
acrylic patina	1. After sanding, rub warm or cool patina into the grain; allow to dry.	2. Rub warm or cool patina over raised surface—try to keep out of holes; when dry rub with fine 000 steel wool until desired effect is achieved.	2. Alternative A: When dry, rub with patina and rub off excess. Rub with Brillo.	4. Alternative A: Brush entire surface with warm and/or cool patina.	

Numbers indicate sequence of steps

Material	Coarse-grained oak, chestnut, spruce, or pine	Wormy Chestnut	Soft woods	Texturing and Finishing	Medium grained, natural effects
acrylic color	2. It is possible to touch accents of color to pick up colors in the picture; allow to set; then steel-wool as much color off as desired.	1. Paint entire frame with dark brown or black acrylic; allow to set, then rub off excess with soft flannel cloth.	2. Alternative B: Paint with desired color. Then try alternative A.	5. Alternative A: Rub 1 or 2 colors over surface. 3. Alternative B: Rub or paint surface with color.	1. Alternative A: Dilute paint with water; brush on evenly and lightly; allow to dry. (optional, when more color is wanted)
acrylic emulsion	3. Brush a thin coat of emulsion over dust-free surface.		2. Alternative C: For gold-leafing, apply a thin coating of emulsion.	5. or 6. Apply a thin coat. (optional)	Alternative C: 1. Brush on several coats of emulsion after each layer is dry; finish by lightly sanding with 300 grit wet-or-dry; wax.
gold leafing			3. Alternative C: With a gilder's brush, transfer gold leaf to almost dry emulsion surface.		
varnish: vinyl, urethane, phenolic or other polymers			4. Alternative C: Optional: Coat 2 or 3 layers of clear varnish over leafed surface; sand smooth, and wax.		Alternative A: 2. Brush varnish on surface; allow to dry thoroughly; after 2nd coat wet-or-dry sand lightly; repeat until 3rd or 4th coat.
paste wax	4. Apply a protective coat of wax (optional).	3. Clean off steel wool with tack cloth; apply a light coating of wax with a soft flannel cloth.	4. Alternatives A & B: Apply a light coat after 1 hour.		3. Alternatives A & C: Apply wax.
linseed oil					1. Alternative B: Steel wool surface; remove grit with tack cloth; rub oil into surface; 3 coats, after each is absorbed.
metallic paste colors			3. Alternatives A & B: With stiff brush, lightly rub metallic paste colors over surface.	4. or 5. Alternative A or B: With fingers, rub metallic paste over raised areas to accent.	

ANTIQUING

Acrylic patina or commercial antiquing medium can be applied with a bristle brush, rag or sponge, or spattered with a brush. Application of antiquing softens edges, distracts from imperfections, and produces a pleasant patina. For the most successful effects, the color of the antiquing must be lighter than the base hue. For example, if the base hue is dark sienna, the antiquing should be at least a medium beige. Another consideration is chromatic intensity: if the base is dark sienna, the antiquing should be a diluted version of the dark sienna, such as a more washed-out version in a beige. Tone can be neutralized no matter what color it is by adding a bit of its complement, or by adding earth colors, such as umber, ochre, etc.

One can achieve a wide variety of effects, depending upon the choice of applicators: a soft or stiff brush, a rag, or a sponge. Rubbing, scraping, dragging, patting, sprinkling—antiquing using any one or even all of these methods will produce endless variety. When using a brush and rag let color dry for a few minutes before rubbing off the excess with a rag. If you wait too long, use sandpaper. You can apply color, sand away color, and reapply more or different colors.

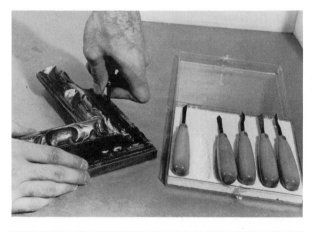

When complex, carved frames are joined, carvings rarely meet and require recarving to effect a better articulation of the joint. Here, a wood-carving tool is used to carve away excess and to match the pattern.

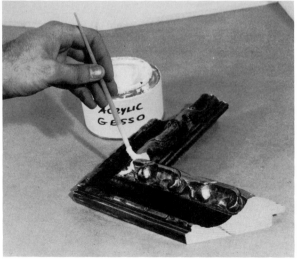

After sanding, two coats of gesso are added.

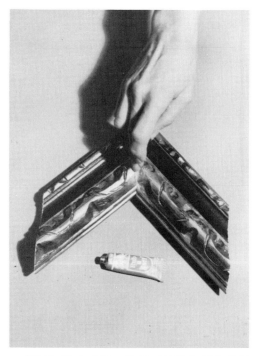

When that dries, it is sanded and then Rub'n Buff "gold leaf" paste is rubbed on.

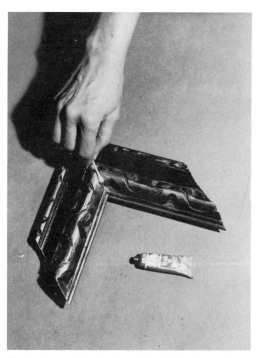

A cotton swab is used to apply the gold paste into corners.

Acrylic in umber, black, or whatever antiquing color had been used on the frame before is rubbed over the surface.

A corner carved and matched to create a continuing pattern.

Refinishing

Inventing is the rule of thumb here. Does your beat-up frame have strong corners? Is it the correct size and width? Will it take countless hours to put it into shape? These will be determinants as to whether it is worthwhile rescuing a frame from the attic, thrift shop, or garbage heap.

PREPARING VARNISHED OR PAINTED WOOD FOR REFINISHING

Varnished wood should be washed with denatured alcohol to remove foreign matter. If the varnish is in fact shellac, the alcohol will remove it. Next sand the surface with 100 garnet paper to provide surface tooth. It is not necessary to expose bare wood, just so long as the surface is roughened. Carving and grooves only need superficial sanding. Then patch any areas that need repair with acrylic modeling paste or a filler. When it dries, sand off any excess. The piece is now ready for a multitude of finishes.

If the frame has paint on it and it is a good job, just sand it with 100 garnet paper until you abrade the surface. A painted horror should have all its paint removed with a heavy-bodied paint remover, following directions on the can. Feather out any chips in the paint with more sanding in that spot. After sanding, wash the frame with denatured alcohol and fill areas that require patching. When that dries, sand away excess and the piece is ready for refinishing.

If the frame is gold-leafed over gesso* and that is over wood, sand away the old leafing with 60-100 garnet paper. Then wash the surface with denatured alcohol. Fill in chips, blemishes, and cracks with acrylic modeling paste or vinyl filler. After it dries, the modeling paste and fillers usually shrink. Apply as many layers as necessary. When dry, sand smooth, if desired. Another alternative is to give a new texture to the entire piece by applying modeling paste with a palette knife. When this has dried thoroughly, sand rough edges, coat the entire piece with one or two applications of acrylic gesso, and when that dries, apply acrylic color.

---

* Gesso can be made, but it is a complicated process to cook it up, and the final product is much inferior to the acrylic or vinyl compositions.

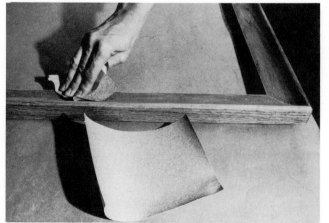

Old wax, varnish, dirt is sanded off. The surface can be rough, have enough tooth to hold an application of modeling paste.

Tack cloth is used to dust away grit.

Acrylic modeling paste is applied with a spatula over the surface generously.

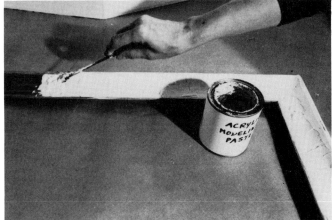

A finger is used to smooth out edges.

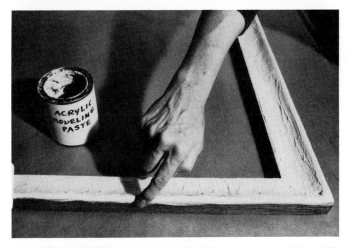

A comb made of plastic, wood, metal, or cardboard can be used to texture the surface.

When the modeling paste hardens, rough raised areas are sanded away with #240 dry sandpaper.

One coat of acrylic gesso is brushed over the surface.

When the gesso dries, the acrylic paint (a warm gray patina) is applied.

And when the acrylic dries, gold paste is lightly touched over raised areas to provide highlights.

The completed frame displaying bark paper fetish forms from Mexico. Other textures are possible with this technique. All one needs to do is experiment with different tools to create new effects.

Novelty Effects

Flat surfaces can be covered with cork, burlap, or other coverings that can be glued to the base surface like the cork-covered frame pictured here. Other cures for old worn-out frames can be to create modeled textures with acrylic modeling paste, as described earlier, or to add papier-mâché to the surface. This is a simple technique, detailed here in step-by-step photos, that has a wide range of possibilities.

Flexible materials such as linen, leather, grass cloth, and felt can also be glued to a flat frame surface. It may be a good idea to add a strip of molding around outside edges to keep fabrics from raveling, if they do not wrap around. Another hint is to spray soilable surfaces with Scotchgard to retard soiling.

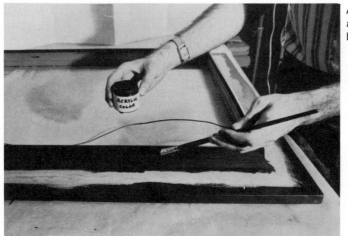

An old frame is prepared and then painted with dark brown acrylic.

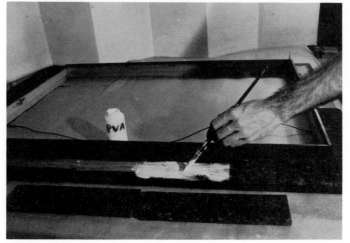

An adhesive, polyvinyl acetate—similar to Elmer's glue or Sobo—is brushed on the areas to receive cork. The cork is measured and cut. And then it is pressed onto the adhesive.

A very simple, but effective technique. *City Lights*, an oil painting, is by Thelma R. Newman.

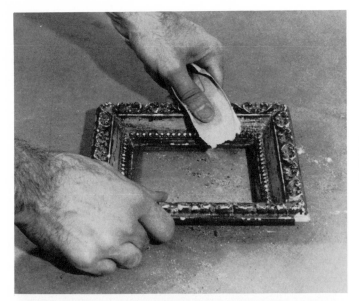

An old chipped frame is sanded and prepared. All loose parts of the finish are sanded away.

A mixture of vinyl wallpaper paste (Metylan) and water is combined following the instructions on the package.

Paper toweling is torn into strips (not cut, because tearing "feathers" the edges), dipped into the paste, and applied to the frame.

After three layers are added, more paper is used as twisted strips for decoration.

A tongue depressor is used to smooth the edges and model the decoration.

After the paper-glue dries, three coats of acrylic-gesso are brushed over the entire frame.

With a stiff bristle brush, a touch of gold paste is used to highlight raised areas followed by some spattering with acrylic raw umber paint.

The completed frame, refurbished into a mirror.

Lois Morrison finds old window and door frames for her trapunto bas relief. She just sands away grime and leaves the natural surface as is.

Novelty Nonframes as Frames

Frames, themselves, are obviously great for framing. But there are also other framing possibilities such as old doorframes with the center panel removed, window frames, wheels with spokes removed; in fact anything that has an opening and a border can work with a bit of imagination. These are great for displays and collections—three-dimensional art and craft forms. Sometimes, if small enough, they can be mounted on a rough, weathered planking background to create a rustic effect. Go easy on finishes when surface textures are exciting. If the wood is weathered, clean it a bit and leave the surface alone. Don't worry about mitering corners; butt joints work well for these novelty effects.

Superimposed Design–Decoupage

If you are framing a picture of a scene, you certainly do not want flowers pasted around the frame. But this might work for a plain mirror frame. You may want to glue an accent or trim in place. Embossed gold foil paper, for instance, will dramatize some aspect in framing. More rarely, there may be some design elements created by the artist that would integrate the frame with the picture. These components may require cutting, gluing, and varnishing, as in decoupage. The process is illustrated here to extend your framing ideas creatively. Decoupage can be serious or frivolous, depending upon how design is approached. Certainly, much could be gained by studying finishing techniques. They can be elegant.

A simple frame, as for this mirror, can be embellished. These embossed paper flowers will be modified to become the decoration.

They are glued into place with a mucilage or PVA glue. Air bubbles are pressed out and light pressure is applied until the flowers are firmly adhered.

Excess glue is washed away with cotton swabs and water.

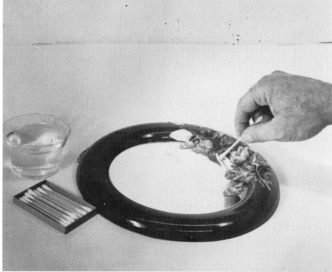

Five coats of varnish are brushed over the whole piece. Each coating has to dry before the next application.

The completed frame with bouquet.

PLASTICS
IN
FRAMING

Plastics have revolutionized many crafts. The use of plastic mediums, paints, and finishes shown in Chapter 4 is evidence of the impact that these materials have had on one part of the framing industry. But plastics have figured importantly as raw framing materials as well as finishes, backing, replacement for glass, etc.

Commercially we have seen new ready-made frame creations of admirable design. The most familiar of these are manufactured by DAX and Structural Industries; they consist of an open-ended plastic box with a white cardboard box filler. Several examples are shown here. And recent additions to this series include recessed and metallized borders that are attractive accents. Frames like these provide convenient means for preserving photographs and small prints. With the addition of a beveled mat—or even a mat cut from a single piece of paper—the results can be quite successful.

The ease with which plastics, especially acrylics, can be machined and formed offers even more room for creative development. Acrylics can be cut and polished easily with machines; and they are an ideal material for the sleek, highly polished, modern look. Acrylics come in a wide range of transparent and opaque colors, and are available in ever-increasing numbers of craft, hardware, and plastics stores. All of them can be glued with a basic solvent cement which is sold wherever the plastic is. The following sequences detail the process involved in working with acrylics as a framing material. A sequence of particular interest shows the use of a strip heater to bend acrylic and form a simple but effective frame which can be adapted to a picture of almost any dimensions. For further references on basic plastic techniques, see the Bibliography.

Besides demonstrating some of the possibilities that acrylic offers the frame maker, a new material available to the custom framer is also included here. For many years the sign industry has used a product called "Jewelite" to make frames for letters which appear in store and building signs. This material is essentially a strip of plastic with a piece of metal embedded within it. The beauty of it is that it can conform to almost any shape that can be cut from acrylic. The stripping is bent around the acrylic "window" and glued with a solvent cement (ethylene dichloride). Circles, ovals, hexagons, indeed any shape is possible with this material. Jewelite is available through many sign makers across the country; many widths and colors are available. The manufacturer will give you the name of regional suppliers upon request. (See Supply Sources in the back of this book.)

Design Considerations

Just as in framing with conventional materials, the design of a frame made with plastics must enhance the subject. Because they are highly polished and modern looking, plastics will not suit every subject, although plastics are excellent for many contemporary expressions. Care must be taken to judge the mood and proportion of an object as you would with any material.

Because many plastic colors are very bright and glossy, colored plastics will only be useful on special occasions. Black, smoke-gray and clear acrylics will have many applications. Because they will not cause the viewer as much distraction as brighter colors, these shades offer strong but not overpowering alternatives.

The use of clear acrylics opens the door to a new concept of framing: frame as structure, protection, and form, all in one. Rather than necessitating the use of separate components (molding, glass, matting, backing) acrylic can form a frame from a single piece, or several pieces, and take the place of everything— including the glass which protects the work of art. (Acrylic sheets have even greater optical clarity than glass of comparable thickness.)

Special qualities of plastics, like moldability, allow fabricators to create globes and bubbles which many custom framers will find intriguing and effective as solutions for novelty items and small, more frivolous things which they might like to protect and emphasize.

The potentialities of plastics as framing materials have barely been examined. The frontiers of this old craft will undoubtedly be expanded by the judicious and creative use of these versatile materials.

Plastic Fabrication Techniques

CUTTING

Acrylic sheets may be purchased already cut to size, or they may be cut to size by the framer himself. Any power saw which will provide a straight edge can be used to cut acrylic. Metal-cutting blades are recommended, since they deliver the sharpest, cleanest cuts. The blade should, preferably, be carbide tipped and have teeth of uniform height. As with any fabrication process, the proper shop precautions should be observed, including the wearing of protective glasses.

POLISHING

The edges can be treated in two ways: they may be dressed or polished. The first steps are the same for both finishes. First, scrape the edge with a wood scraper to remove any deep pits or scratches which may have resulted from sawing. Then sand the edge with a succession of wet-or-dry sandpapers, going from coarse grit (150) to a finer grit (220) and then to the finest (400). The result is called a "dressed" edge which is a matte, translucent surface.

For certain frames you will not want a glossy surface. In that case a dressed edge should be chosen. You may want to experiment by fine-sanding the *face* of the acrylic, too. This will result in a dulled surface which will extend the vocabulary of acrylic in framing, since a high polish is not suitable for all works.

If a high polish is desired, best results will be achieved with a two-wheel electric buffer. The buffs should be loosely bound 10″ diameter muslin revolving at 200 surface feet per minute. One buff should be used with a white tripoli buffing compound to remove any scratches from the edges. Only light pressure is necessary to clear the surface of the shallow sanding grooves. The second buffing wheel should be left clean; use it to remove excess compound and to buff the acrylic to a high shine.

Do not be deterred by a lack of elaborate machinery, however. Excellent results can be achieved with a buffing wheel attached to an electric hand drill (such wheels often come as optional accessories for drills). Just be certain that your wheel is not revolving too fast. If it is, the plastic will melt and gum up from the heat of friction.

GLUING

The best glue for adhering acrylic is a solvent cement, ethylene dichloride. It is readily available wherever acrylic is sold. The application of this cement utilizes the natural principle of capillary action. That is to say, after you align the two pieces you want glued, all you need to do is draw a brush filled with solvent along the edge and the cement will be drawn into the joint, creeping across the crack. Since solvent evaporates quickly, most joints will set in a few minutes, although full strength will not be reached for several hours.

Acrylic is probably the best known type of plastic. Although invented nearly forty years ago, it is just coming into its own as a crafts medium. Recognized most often by the trade names of Lucite (Du Pont), Plexiglas (Rohm & Haas), Acrylite (American Cyanamid), Perspex (Imperial Chemical Industries, Ltd.), this thermoplastic is outstanding for crafts use because of its versatility and the ease with which it can be formed and machined. To mark the plastic before cutting—and to protect it from scratches—acrylic sheets come with a paper covering. Marks can be made in pencil and pen on this paper as guides for cutting. If it is necessary to make marks directly on the acrylic use a grease pencil. The first step here is to cut a piece of ⅛″ thick black acrylic to the basic size for the frame.

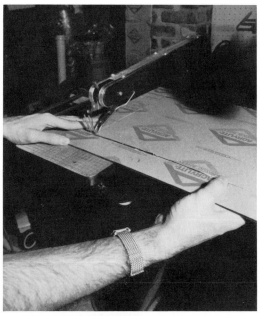

Power tools of almost any sort are suitable for cutting acrylic. Radial arm saws, band saws, table saws, jigsaws, saber saws are all appropriate. Metal-cutting blades deliver the cleanest results. Only be certain that the blade does not revolve too fast; if it does the friction may cause the plastic to overheat and gum up. The jigsaw being used here is especially useful for cutting in tight or enclosed areas.

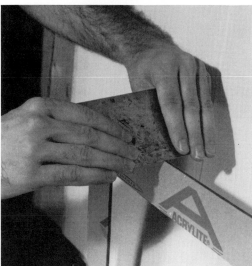

To finish the edges of acrylic, begin by scraping them with a sharp metal scraper. This tool is used in woodworking, but it is emminently applicable to plastics. Scraping removes surface scratches and roughness from manufacturing and cutting operations. Use long smooth strokes, otherwise you might create a "belly" or uneven area along an edge. The frame being constructed here is made with a single top piece of acrylic with a window cut out of its center. Four strips are later added around its edges to create a box for the picture to sit in.

After scraping, wet-sand the edges. This will create a matte sheen known as a "dressed" edge. The dressed edge is often used as the final finish, but for our purposes the process is continued through to the polishing stage. When sanding, begin with coarser papers and work to finer grits until the surface becomes very smooth. Allow the protective paper to remain on the plastic during these processes.

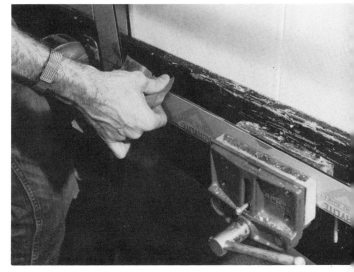

After scraping and sanding, the edges may be polished and buffed to a high shine. Use a fine compound, such as diamond-based buffing compound. Your buffing wheel may range from the professional three step system (in which one wheel holds a coarse compound, another holds a fine compound, and a third is for buffing the plastic clean), the two step setup we show here, or simply a buffer at the end of an electric drill. All will serve you well. The only guide that should be followed fairly closely is to make certain that the buffing wheel turns at a speed that will not overheat the acrylic (usually not more than 1750 RPM).

A strong, almost invisible bond can be made when cementing acrylic to acrylic. Some of the best results can be obtained by using a solvent cement like ethylene dichloride or methylene dichloride. The solvent cement should be applied with a brush, eyedropper, or hypodermic-type needle. Cement need not be applied to both surfaces to be bonded. It can be introduced to the joints after the acrylic pieces have been butted together through capillary action. Here, the face of our frame was clamped to a table which had a strip of wood nailed to it at a right angle to the table's surface—acting as a jig. A side panel to this frame was then clamped to the wood strip so that one edge butted against the back of the frame face. A brush charged with solvent cement was drawn along the joint, and the cement was drawn into that joint by capillary action. The bond is firm in five minutes and cures in about an hour.

The three other sides were adhered similarly, and small rectangles of clear acrylic (it could have been any color since they will not be seen in the final instance) were added to support the picture in the frame. Once again, after the pieces were set in place, a cement-laden brush was drawn along the joint allowing solvent cement to enter and join the plastic.

To firmly anchor the picture in the frame, two strips of acrylic were added across the back. The overall structure of this frame is visible here: the box of acrylic, corners to support the picture, and back supports to keep the picture from falling out.

For comparison, the painting, *Carnival,* by Phillip Moore, is shown here as it looked before framing. Although it did have a recessed box frame, the effect left something to be desired, since the painting needed to be focused better.

Black acrylic makes a world of difference. The white recession was allowed to remain, with our black box strongly defining the space around the painting, making it more visible—without competing for attention.

HEAT FORMING

Heat forming is a technique for shaping acrylics which employs a quality peculiar to these thermoplastics. Thermoplastics are giant molecules which were originally created by heat and pressure and which will become soft and pliable again when subjected to heat.

Acrylic may be heated as a sheet—in which case the piece may be molded and shaped in any way you desire. It may also be heated along a single line with the use of the strip heater. The strip heating technique will provide the framer with a versatile style of framing. By aligning a piece of acrylic over (but not touching) a heating element, the acrylic will be softened along that single line. It can then be bent to create a frame like the one shown in the following pages. Strip heating elements and instructions for building a simple strip heater are available at many hardware and craft stores.

Freestanding Acrylic Picture Frame

This freestanding acrylic picture frame, attractive for its simplicity and compatibility with any decor, is one of the easiest frames to make. The only prerequisite is a strip heater for acrylic. A strip heater can be built simply and inexpensively. Follow the instructions on the back of the Briskeat RH-36 heating element (sold in many hardware and plastics stores). The address is included in the Sources of Supply section. More detailed instructions can be found in *Plastics for the Craftsman.**

After determining the size of the clear acrylic sheet and cutting it, scrape, sand, and polish the edges of the rectangle. Peel off the protective paper and mark the length of the plastic in thirds, using a ruler and grease pencil. (The marks can be rubbed off with a soft cloth after lining up the acrylic over the strip heating element.)

Lay the acrylic over the heating element by centering the marking. Allow the plastic to heat thoroughly. You will know it is soft enough to be bent when the acrylic changes its texture slightly or welts occur in the forming area.

Gently bend the plastic with the heated side out until it meets the longer part of the original strip. It is essential that the heated part of the acrylic be on the outside of the bend. The piece should be held flush against the other acrylic as snugly as possible to form a 180° angle at the joint. Since pictures will be inserted in this acrylic sandwich later on, the bend should be made fairly tight.

Hold the acrylic in this position until it cools. It is important to note that bending the acrylic before it is completely heated will result in internal fractures (crazing) along the bend.

When the acrylic bend has cooled, put the piece across the strip heater again, this time with the other grease pencil mark centered over the element. The shorter end of the acrylic sandwich should be facing up, since it is meant to become the back of the frame (see photographs).

After sufficiently heating this joint, bend it to an approximate 60° angle to the sandwich part, forming the stand for the picture holder. Hold this joint until it is cool. Use alcohol or a spray wax applied with a soft rag to clean the frame.

* By Jay Hartley Newman and Lee Scott Newman, Crown Publishers, Inc., 1972.

All that now remains to be done is to slide a photograph or print into the acrylic sandwich. This idea can be adapted in a number of ways. A double frame, in which two sandwiches are folded, may be made. It can stand on its side, or corner. And, by making the opening a little wider during the forming process, room can be allowed for the insertion of a mat and backing as well as the artwork.

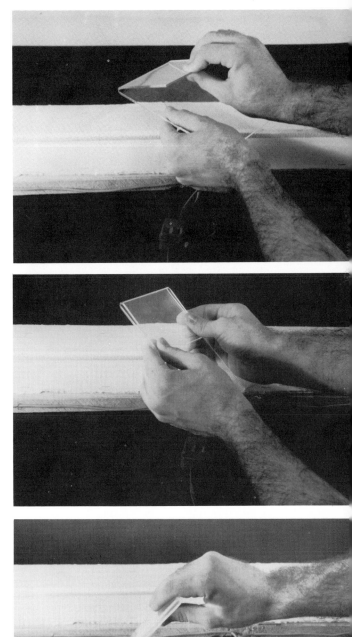

When the heated area begins to welt, it is ready for bending. Bend the acrylic gently, and make certain that the heated area is on the outside of the bend.

Fold the plastic back onto itself and hold it in place until it cools. If desired, space may be allowed to accommodate a mat or mounting board.

Follow the same procedure for the second bend which will form the base of the frame. When the acrylic is sufficiently pliable, fold it back to form a 60° angle.

With only two heatings and bendings, one to form a 180° sandwich of acrylic and another to create a base at a 60° angle to the face of the frame, the picture holder is completed. As you can see, the completed frame is ready for *any* picture.

Acrylic Display Boxes

Acrylic has one "framing" advantage that no other material can offer. Because it can be machined, polished, and adhered so easily, acrylic can be used to construct transparent boxes for objects which could not be easily displayed otherwise. Witness the special box constructed here to display a pair of precious obsidian earrings.

Black, clear, and mirrored acrylic were combined to construct a fine, small box which would house these delicate objects without detracting from the marvelous translucency that makes them so special.

The first step is always the same: cut the acrylic to size. In this case, four pieces of clear acrylic were cut to the same size as sides for this box, and a top was cut from clear plastic as well. Four strips and a top were cut from black acrylic for the base of this box. The sizes and proportion of top to base are not specified because you will want to decide upon those in relation to whatever object is being housed.

The sanding and polishing processes are carried out, and the gluing is done as well. The special exception to this basic process involves the use of mirrored acrylic and two small sections of acrylic rod on which to "mount" the earrings.

A piece of mirrored acrylic was cut a size smaller than the top of the black plastic base. The mirror should be smaller so that the top section of clear acrylic will fit over it and be held in place by the mirrored acrylic—in reverse of the rabbet of a frame. The mirror is adhered to the base with double-stick carpet tape, because the solvents in most adhesives will attack the mirror. Two half-inch sections of acrylic rod were cemented onto the mirror to hold the two hollow earrings in place.

ACRYLIC DISPLAY BOX
After cutting, scrape the acrylic with a woodworking metal scraper.

Wet-sand the edges after scraping. Progress from coarse grit paper (150) to finer grits.

Then polish the edges on a buffing wheel or with a buffer attached to an electric drill.

After the base has been completed, here in black acrylic, attach the cut and polished piece of acrylic mirror with double-stick carpet tape. Press the tape onto the underside of the mirror and trim away the excess. When working with mirrored acrylic, always be careful not to scratch the coated underside. And remember that once the tape has been applied it cannot be removed without removing the mirror coating—so be careful and be precise!

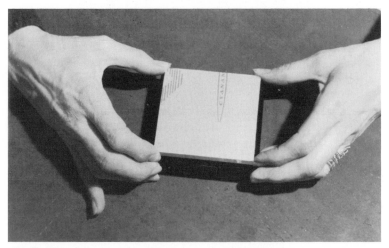

Peel away the paper from the other side of the tape, and carefully place the piece of mirror on its base. Then remove the protective paper to reveal a perfect reflection.

The gluing process is carried on for the top section as previously shown. Allow capillary action to do some work for you. Align the pieces of acrylic and draw a solvent-bearing brush along the joint. Cement will rush in and bond the pieces together. Either clamp the pieces firmly beforehand or be prepared to hold them together for a few minutes until the glue sets.

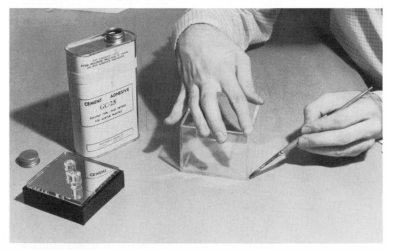

Two half-inch sections of acrylic rod were cemented to the mirror surface in order to support the earrings. As you can see, this box admirably serves the purpose it set out to fulfill. The contents are visible, attractively housed, and the box is functional and appealing without denying the real beauty of its contents. This basic concept of box building can be used for any size display case.

The Plastic Potential

As you can see, the use of plastics requires the application of new, but simple, procedures. And as with any material that can be easily machined, shaped, polished, and glued, the possibilities will be much greater than anyone could enumerate. A little experience with plastics will bring to mind many more design ideas.

JEWELITE FRAMES

To construct frames with Jewelite, begin by cutting a piece of clear, ⅛″ acrylic to size. Fit the acrylic into the rabbet and mark the end of the sheet with the edge of a small file.

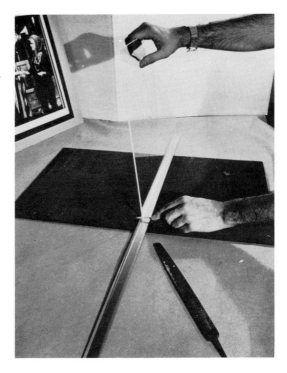

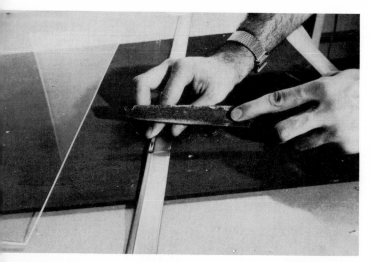

Then, with a larger file—preferably one with a square corner—file the Jewelite so that a wedge of 90° is cut out.

This will allow the material to be bent squarely. After each filing, bend the Jewelite as shown here so that it begins to conform to the proper angle.

The stripping may be glued to the acrylic after each side is readied or all at once. Here one side is glued at a time. The acrylic is laid in the rabbet and solvent glue is applied.

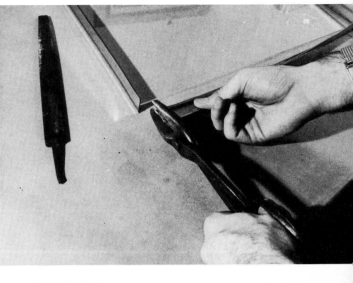

When you reach the end, use heavy scissors or nippers to trim away excess stripping.

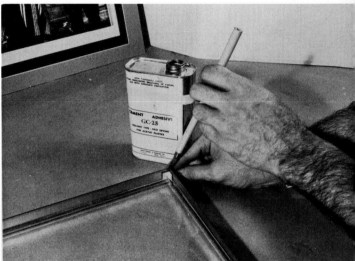

Cut a small piece of Jewelite and add it as reinforcement at the corner where the ends meet. If possible, each frame should be made from a single piece of stripping.

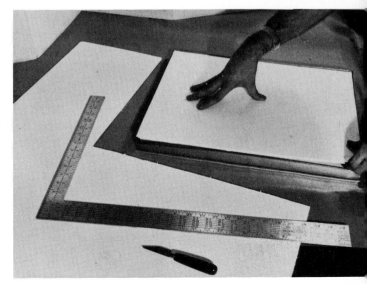

A piece of foam core board is fitted into the back of the frame to firmly secure the matted photograph which was placed in first.

The final piece shows the hinged mat which was cut and assembled in Chapter 2. This is a very successful frame; it is attractive, but unassuming— it allows the strong colors of the photograph and matting to stand out.

By far the most interesting possibility that Jewelite offers the frame craftsman is the opportunity to make curved and round frames—or frames with convoluted shapes. A circle of acrylic forms the basis for the frame shown. It is being cut on a Dremel jigsaw.

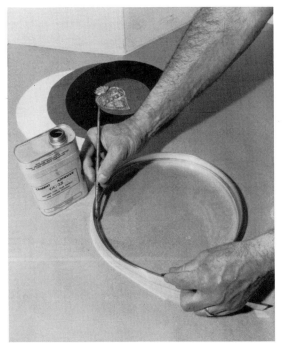

In order to form and fit the stripping, bend it into a coil and hold it that way for a few minutes. This will curl it into a curve of sorts. Then fit the circular piece of acrylic into the rabbet. Bend the stripping around the plastic, and apply the solvent cement. Hold the stripping in place while the glue sets. Then trim and attach the ends of the stripping the same as above, with a little tab of stripping as a joiner. Mat, mount, and backing may then be added.

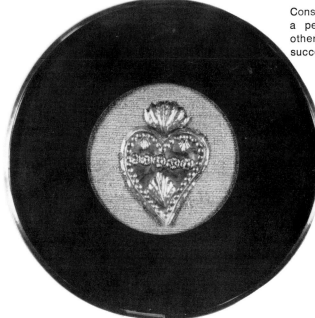

Considering the difficulty of making a perfectly round frame with any other material, this is a fantastic success!

Commercial plastic frames such as this FLOAT FRAME by DAX offer exciting possibilities as well. The components: a mounted print, plastic box, paperboard insert, and floating frame.

The framed print by Carl Burger shows how elegant and satisfying the "boughten" frame can be.

GALLERY
OF
NOVELTY FRAMES

Novelty viewed as an attractive design idea for a frame would be an anachronism here because we believe that a frame is a setting for the work of art that it is displaying—and not the attraction itself. But novelty can be thought of in terms of other kinds of material than wood—leather, ceramic, metal, and so on.

Leather can be employed as a covering over wood. When it is simply a covering meant to evoke the sensuous quality so characteristic of leather, it is effective. Or when heavy leather is the structure of a frame, independent of wood, the result is again quite satisfying. But when, as in one illustration shown here, leather is embroidered on leather, the effect is dynamic. The frame is what you appreciate.

Metal, too, can impose a challenge. Although some of the most successful frames are simple aluminum structures (these are sold in every art store and most museum stores), it takes a very lucky combination of elements to successfully combine an ornate silver repoussé frame and the art work itself. Because the antique Spanish silver repoussé frame illustrated here has an even more exotic and colorful Guatemalan wedding veil, the marriage works. A delicate pastel portrait, however, would be lost, if framed in such an ornate and precious setting.

Papier-mâché, as another decorative frame, can be simple or grossly ornate, depending upon design. As described earlier, papier-mâché can refurbish a worn-out frame. But frames can also be made from scratch completely of paper, papier-mâché over a base of a box, or over an armature such as carpenter's cloth which is a metal meshlike grid. Use of plastic adhesives such as vinyl (Metylan) with paper makes for permanence which can be ensured further by using many coatings of plastic paints and/or varnishes.

Ceramic has potential as a framing material, but because of weight, size is a limitation. Most ceramic frames are small and are used as decorative settings for mirrors. Only if a large ceramic frame were permanently attached to a wall could it frame a work of art. Here is where we would come full-cycle, back to man's first frames which were actually architectural elements.

This leather frame, embroidered with leather strips, designed by Ed Ghossn for L'Insolite, is self-important—too dynamic to frame anything but a mirror image.

An antique Spanish silver repoussé frame defines an even more dynamic Guatemalan brightly colored silk-embroidered wedding veil. The two harmonize because of a style-period relationship.

Based on cardboard boxes, these two papier-mâché frames are decorative, excellent frames for mirrors.

A free-standing frame that encloses a portrait. To change the picture, all one needs to do is to unbuckle the strap which is the frame itself. By Richard Rosengarten.

Leather frames such as these are simple to make. Two layers of leather are hammered together with clinching nails (used by the shoemaker) over metal. (The nail embeds back into the leather.) The parallel line around the inside of the frame is carved with a linoleum cutting tool. By Ed Viola.

Another leather frame is a mirror wrapped with leather and hung with a beltlike strap. By Richard Rosengarten.

A novelty frame, hand carved and painted in bright enamel colors over wood. It functions very well as a mirror.

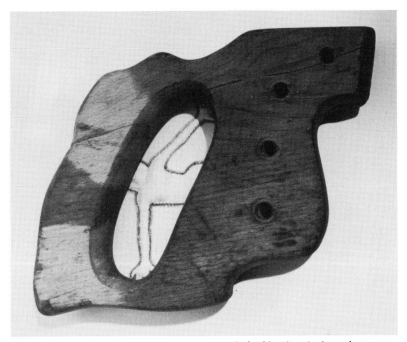

Lois Morrison's ingenious use of an old saw handle as a frame for her trapunto art work.

Another reclaimed frame by Lois Morrison. This time it is half of a window frame.

Gesso coated over modeling paste provides the decorative pattern for this brown antiqued frame. The base is wood. In this case the modeled pattern is not so busy as to severely limit its enclosure.

A Mexican tin frame made of tin wire that is soldered to ball-like tin elements in a repeat design. It presently encloses a mirror, but would be suitable for a very dynamic, brightly colored folk art piece.

Small ceramic frames illustrating four variations on a theme. Note that one is hung with leather thonging.

A ceramic frame in a neutral gray glaze that has a shallow relief design. It is small. A large ceramic form would require permanent attachment to a wall. This would come full-circle to man's first frames, which were architectural elements.

BIBLIOGRAPHY

Bauhof, Ellwood, and Chapin, Robert C., Jr., *Handmade Picture Frames from Simple Moldings*. Philadelphia, Pa.: Countryside Press, 1971.

Burnett, Janet and Laurence, *The Picture Framer's Handbook*. N.Y.: Clarkson N. Potter, Inc., 1973.

Heydenryk, Henry, *The Right Frame*. N.Y.: James H. Heineman, Inc., 1963.

Hyder, Max, *Picture Framing*. N.Y.: Pitman Publishing Corp., 1963.

Keck, Caroline K., *How to Take Care of Your Pictures*. N.Y.: The Museum of Modern Art, 1965.

Newman, Jay Hartley and Lee Scott, *Plastics for the Craftsman*. N.Y.: Crown Publishers, Inc., 1972.

Newman, Thelma R., *Contemporary Decoupage*. N.Y.: Crown Publishers, Inc., 1972.

———, *Leather as Art and Craft*. N.Y.: Crown Publishers, Inc., 1973.

Newman, Thelma R., Jay Hartley, and Lee Scott, *Paper as Art and Craft*. N.Y.: Crown Publishers, Inc., 1973.

O'Neil, Isabel, *The Art of the Painted Finish*. N.Y.: William Morrow & Company, Inc., 1971.

Taubes, Frederic, *Better Frames for Your Pictures*. N.Y.: The Viking Press, 1968.

Toscano, Eamon, *Step-by-Step Framing*. N.Y.: Golden Press, 1971.

GLOSSARY

ACRYLIC
: a synthetic resin formed under heat and pressure into sheets, tubes, and rods. Also made into fast-drying paints. Acrylic comes in a variety of colors and finishes including mirrored, clear, smoke-gray, rippled. Common trade names for the acrylic sheets include Plexiglas, Lucite, Acrylite.

ADHESIVE MOUNT
: a technique of attaching prints to mounts using a sticky film as adhesive.

ANTIQUING
: a way of making a frame look old, creating an artificial patina. This type of finish for a frame is often made by applying a commercial antiquing medium to a darker color frame, or else using acrylic paint to imitate patina with soft streaks and spatter, diluting the intensity of the base color and value.

BEVEL
: the angle at which mats are cut (i.e., toward the subject or away from it). Also, a slanted edge or side of a molding strip.

BUILDER'S MOLDING
: molding strips available at lumberyards, generally used as house trimming. It is highly adaptable to picture framing by the simple addition of a parting strip rabbet to the molding's back face.

COUNTERMOUNT
: a piece of paper attached to the back of a mounted print.

COUNTERSINKING
: the driving of nails below the surface of the frame molding, using a nail set and a hammer.

CRABS
: a frame maker's colloquialism for lint and debris that accumulates on cloth mats and liners.

DECOUPAGE

the employment of reproductions or paper forms as cutouts, which are pasted, varnished, and sanded until the original decoration is completely embedded.

DRESSED EDGE AND POLISHED EDGE

a dressed acrylic sheet edge has been scraped with a wood scraper, and been finely sanded smooth. A polished edge goes one step beyond dressing, calling for the use of an electric polishing wheel to buff the ends and edges until transparent like the face of the acrylic.

DRY MOUNT

the use of heat/pressure-activated film which comes coated with a plastic adhesive. This film is used in the mounting of a print, photograph, or other fragile subjects that require the firmness of a mat in framing.

EMBOSSING

the process of raising an area above the flat surface. Also see *Repoussé*.

ETHYLENE DICHLORIDE

the solvent cement used to bond acrylic sheets together.

FILLETS

wood spacers used in combination frames and shadow boxes as a partition. Also, a second inner mat on a mat of contrasting color or metal leaf.

FINISHING

treatment of raw woods with color, metal leaf, antiquing processes, gesso, etc., to change the appearance of the molding strips.

FRAME

a border or case for enclosing an object or picture, the standard of which is made from wood molding strips, cut on a miter box, joined with nails and glue, and otherwise finished with paints, lacquers, and waxes.

FRAME SIGHT SIZE

the dimensions of a picture which can be seen after the frame has been set over it. A type of measurement in frame making which is generally ignored in favor of the rabbet size. See *Rabbet Size*.

GESSO

a painting ground or base that acts as a sealer and painting surface for colorants. In this book a polymer medium (plastic) gesso is indicated. It can also be mixed with acrylic paint to form a thick colorant and filler. Also used as gesso are gypsum or plaster of Paris prepared with glue for use as a surface painting.

GILDER'S TIP

the brush used to pick up and lay down gold and metal leaf.

GILDING (GOLD AND METAL LEAFING)

the process of applying pounded sheets of thin metal to frames and other surfaces, attaching with an adhesive which is first applied to the wood. Gold leaf is a form of exceedingly thin foil 4–5 millionths of an inch thick and made of pure or synthetic gold. Gilding may employ such gold sheets or may be considered a gold painting process as well.

GRAIN

the texture of the wood, made up of fine or coarse lines that follow a common direction.

GUILLOTINE

a hand or electric tool, also called a "chopper," used for cutting 45° mitered edges. It makes a clean cut of molding strips with one or two strokes.

INSERT

any molding strip used inside an outer frame to form a transition between that outer molding and the picture itself; i.e., a liner is an insert.

LINER

an insert which is a wooden frame molding usually covered with linen, fabric, or metal leaf. Size of liners ranges from ⅜″ to over 6″. It is usually a transitional element in the art of frame making.

MAT

any of a number of colored, textured, or cloth-covered sheets with a window cut out for showing the picture. Usually made of cardboard base, the mat protects the subject from direct contact with the glass, serves a decorative function, and focuses attention on the subject.

MATTE AND GLOSSY

a matte surface is dull and nonreflective. Glossy surfaces have shine and sheen.

METYLAN

a vinyl paste for paperhanging.

MITER BOX

a framing tool used in conjunction with a backsaw to cut mitered corners in molding strips. Most miter boxes, while able to cut 45° angles, can also cut other angles for hexagonal, octagonal, diamond-shaped, or other abnormal custom frame designs.

MODELING PASTE

a plastic ground which can be used to create relief patterns or, when mixed with acrylic color, can be used to fill cracks and countersunk holes in frames.

MOUNTING BOARD

used to preserve fragile or thin subjects that require additional support in framing, the mounting board serves as a backing and is usually made of Upson, temlock, or new foam core board.

OPAQUE

nontransparent.

OVAL AND CIRCULAR FRAMES

mostly manufactured in Europe, oval and circular frames require special techniques beyond the range of most framers. Available in standard sizes from frame stores. While curved shapes are not easily made in wood, they can be made with Jewelite.

PAPIER-MÂCHÉ

a substance consisting of paper pulp or paper mixed with wheat paste and shaped by molding it. As a technique, it produces simple, lightweight frames and decorations which can be painted over with acrylic paints.

PARTING STRIPS

wood strips usually found in standard sizes of ½″ × ¾″ and used to form the rabbet on builder's molding.

PASSE-PARTOUT

an inexpensive, temporary framing technique using glass, plain backing, and mount to sandwich the print, sealed in with plastic tape.

PATINA

a surface finish for wood or metal found on objects grown beautiful with age or use. Patina can be imitated with some finishing techniques described in the text.

PICTURE FRAME MOLDING

wood strips made especially for framing which have built-in rabbets and come in a variety of bevels and curves.

PICTURE GLASS

the thin glass (usually 16-ounce) used in framing. It has greater optical clarity than plate glass or the special nonreflective glass. Acrylic sheets may also be used.

POLYVINYL ACETATE (PVA)

the all-purpose white glue used liberally in most framing processes; commonly known as Elmer's Glue-All or Sobo Glue.

PREFINISHED MOLDINGS

molding strips which are already finished in gold leaf, paint, lacquer, or other special finishes. If the framer chooses this shortcut he need only touch up the completed frame at the joints and nail holes.

PRESSURE-SENSITIVE TAPE

a double-faced tape, sticky on both sides, used to bond mats to prints in instances when glue should not be applied.

PROFILES

the curves and bevels peculiar to each type of molding design—judged by the cross-section or "profile" of the molding bar.

RABBET

the extension at the back of a frame into which the picture must sit. A rabbet holds picture, mat, mount, glass, etc., in place.

RABBET SIZE

the key measurement in all framing. It is the dimension of the rabbet (as opposed to the inner frame sight size). The rabbet size is usually made fractionally larger than the actual picture or mount size, in order to accommodate the subject easily but snugly.

REPOUSSÉ

a shallow relief much like bas-relief that shapes the material so that it projects away from a base.

RIGHT ANGLE

a 90° angle formed by perpendicular lines—all mitered and joined rectangular frame corners should form right angles.

SHADOW BOX
a type of combination frame which requires depth to support three-dimensional objects behind glass.

SOLVENT
a substance that dissolves other substances. See *Ethylene Dichloride.*

SPATTER
sprinkled India ink used to neutralize color and value of a finish. Also, diluted acrylic paint can be used in a spatter technique.

STRETCHER BARS
most canvases, before being painted on, are stretched on interlocking bars. The bars keep the cloth taut, and the canvas should be left on them. Compensation in the depth of the rabbet should be made for the stretcher bars' thickness.

STRIP HEATER
an electric heating element encased in asbestos strips which is used to soften acrylic. By softening (through heat) one line in an acrylic sheet, the sheet can easily be bent and shaped.

STRIPPING OR BATTEN
another name for builder's molding without rabbet.

THERMOPLASTICS
synthetic materials that will soften when heated and harden when cooled. A thermoplastic material may be repeatedly heated, softened, and reshaped (see *Strip Heater, Acrylic*).

TRIMMING
thin molding, usually gold or silver in color, embossed, or beaded, is used as decoration which, when placed inside another molding, serves to define an area or accent some part of the frame design.

VARNISH
the overall term that covers transparent coatings and includes lacquers as well.

WARM AND COOL
a way of talking about the range of visible colors; warm hues have reds mixed in them (i.e., crimsons, burnt umber) while cool colors have blue in them (i.e., raw umber, turquoise).

WET MOUNT
a technique of mounting which is important only in preserving and restoring damaged, bent, or crumpled subjects.

SOURCES
OF
SUPPLY

ACRYLIC SHEETING

Ain Plastics
65 Fourth Avenue
New York, N.Y. 10003

Industrial Plastics
324 Canal Street
New York, N.Y. 10013

Studio Plastique
W. H. Glover, Inc.
171 First Avenue
Atlantic Highlands, N.J. 07716

And any place where plastics are sold.
Look up "plastics" in the Yellow Pages
of your telephone directory.

ADHESIVES

Barge Cement Division
National Starch & Chemical Corp.
100 Jacksonville Road
Towaco, N.J. 07082
    Barge.

Borden Chemical Co.
360 Madison Avenue
New York, N.Y. 10017
    Elmer's Glue.

Harrower House
River Road
Upper Black Eddy
Bucks County, Pa. 18972
    Mucilage for decoupage.

Miracle Adhesive Corp.
Bellmore, N.Y. 11710
    Water clear epoxy.

Slomons Labs, Inc.
32–45 Hunter's Point Avenue
Long Island City, N.Y. 11101
    Sobo, Quik. Also sold in stationery
    stores, five-and-tens, hardware
    stores, paint stores, and arts &
    crafts stores.

3M Company
St. Paul, Minn. 55119
    3M Spra-ment rubber cement.

Tra-Con, Inc.
55 North Street
Medford, Mass. 02155
    Clear, water-white epoxy.

COLORINGS: PAINT AND SPECIAL FINISHES

American Art Clay Company, Inc.
4010 W. 96th Street
Indianapolis, Ind. 46268
    Easy Leaf (synthetic gold leaf),
    Rub'n'Buff.

American Crayon Company
Sandusky, Ohio 44870
    Prang acrylic paint.

Barrett Varnish Company
1532 South 50th Street
Cicero, Ill. 60650
    Exotic spray paints that produce
    a speck and spun gold effect.

H. Behlen & Bros., Inc.
P.O. Box 698
Amsterdam, N.Y. 12010
    Everything for wood finishing—a
    complete line and a very good
    source.

Connoisseur Studios
Box 7187
Louisville, Ky. 40207
    Treasure Gold.

Deft
Torrance, Calif. 90503
    Varnish.

Hunt Manufacturing Company
1405 Locust Street
Philadelphia, Pa. 19102
    Vanguard acrylic paints, emul-
    sions, and modeling pastes.

McCloskey's Varnishes
Philadelphia, Pa. 19136
    McCloskey's Heirloom Varnish.

N.Y. Bronze Powder Company
519 Dowd Avenue
Elizabeth, N.J. 07201
    Polyurethane spray.

Permanent Pigments
27000 Highland Avenue
Cincinnati, Ohio 45212
    Liquitex acrylic paint, emulsions,
    and modeling paste.

CORK

Bradley Enterprises
Main Street
Bradley Beach, N.J. 07720

Dodge Cork Company
Lancaster, Pa. 17604

FRAMES: READYMADE & SYSTEMS

Art Infinitum, Inc.
422 E. 92nd Street
New York, N.Y. 10028
    The DAX® frame. DAX® One/Two
    float frames.

Kulicke Frames
43 E. 10th Street
New York, N.Y. 10003

Structural Industries, Inc.
96 New South Road
Hicksville, N.Y. 11801
    The Frame Pak, Instant Frame,
    Frame-Up/Frame-It: aluminum sec-
    tion frames, C-Thru Frame, In-
    sight Frame, Welded Frame, Ob-
    ject Box.

JEWELITE

Jewelite Letters
13 East 31st Street
New York, N.Y. 10016
    Request information on the sup-
    plier in your area. Plastic strip-
    ping for frame making.

LEATHER

Charles Horowitz & Sons, Inc.
25 Great Jones Street
New York, N.Y.

Saks Arts & Crafts
207 N. Milwaukee Street
Milwaukee, Wisc. 53202

Tandy Leather Company Stores
(Look in the Yellow Pages for the one
nearest you.)

MATS, MOUNTS, BACKINGS

Charles T. Bainbridge's Sons
20 Cumberland Street
Brooklyn, N.Y. 11205
    The most complete line of mats
    and boards including fabric, cork,
    antique, tone, pebbled boards, and
    foam core boards.

Bienfang Paper Company
P.O. Box 408
Metuchen, N.J. 08840
    Manufacturers of mat board,
    foam core, backing boards, and
    DUO-MATS: mats in precut stand-
    ard sizes with a different color
    on each side.

W. F. R. Ribbon Corp.
583 Avenue of the Americas
New York, N.Y. 10011
> Crushed velvet, burlap, velour with adhesive and nonadhesive backings.

MISCELLANEOUS

Hobby Hill, Inc.
417 North State Street
Chicago, Ill. 60610
> Hang-O-Lite picture lights.

Photo Associates
P.O. Box 2038-R
Morristown, N.J. 07960
> Double-stick film for adhesive mounting of photographs and prints.

S & W Framing Supplies
431 Wills Avenue
Williston Park, N.Y. 11596
> A complete line for framing findings and tools.

Three Star Manufacturing
20665 W. Santa Clara Street
Saugus, Calif. 91350
> Stretcher bars.

MOLDINGS

Moldings are available from lumber-yards and specialists in every part of the country. Frame stores often sell small quantities of moldings.

Bendix Mouldings, Inc.
235 Pegasus Avenue
Northvale, N.J. 07647
> A complete line of finished wood moldings, circular and oval frames, and metal-clad moldings.

Craftsman Wood Service
2727 S. Mary Street
Chicago, Ill. 60608
> Carved wood moldings.

Dykes Lumber Company
1901 Park Avenue
Weehawken, N.J. 07087
> A wide range of unfinished construction moldings, rabbeted and unrabbeted.

Piedmont Moulding Company
P.O. Box 117
Conyers, Ga. 30207
> A complete line of finished moldings and findings.

Poly-Dec Company, Inc.
P.O. Box 541
Bayonne, N.J. 07002
> Precut pieces and lengths of molding for craftsmen, mail-order.

PAPIER-MÂCHÉ MIXES

Activa Products, Inc.
7 Front Street
San Francisco, Calif. 94111
> Celluclay instant papier-mâché.

Henkel, Inc.
Teaneck, N.J. 07666
> Metylan paste. Available at places where paint and wallpaper supplies are sold.

Riverside Paper Corp.
Appleton, Wisc. 54911
> Décomâché.

SANDPAPERS AND POLISHING COMPOUNDS

H. Behlen & Bros., Inc.
P.O. Box 698
Amsterdam, N.Y. 12010

The Butcher Polish Company
Boston, Massachusetts 02158
> Butcher's white diamond wax.

Hyprez Diamond Compounds
Engis Corporation
8035 N. Austin Avenue
Morton Grove, Ill. 60053

Matchless Metal Polish Company
Glen Ridge, N.J. 07028
> Buffing compound.

Norton Company
Coated Abrasive Division
Troy, N.Y. 12181
> Tufbak-Durite, wet-or-dry abrasive paper.

Rockland Dental Co., Inc.
S.E. Corner 21st & Clearfield Sts.
Philadelphia, Pa. 19132
> Flex-i-Grit, aluminum oxide coated Mylar abrasive.

SOLVENT CEMENTS FOR ACRYLICS

Ain Plastics
65 Fourth Avenue
New York, N.Y. 10003

Dick Blick
Box 1267
Galesburg, Ill. 61401

Industrial Plastics
324 Canal Street
New York, N.Y. 10013

National Solvent Corp.
3751 Jennings Road
Cleveland, Ohio 44109

Saks Arts & Crafts
207 N. Milwaukee Street
Milwaukee, Wisc. 53202

And anywhere that acrylic sheeting is sold. Look up "plastics" in the Yellow Pages.

STRIP HEATING ELEMENT

Briscol Mfg. Co.
1055 Gibbart
Columbus, Ohio 43216
 Briskeat RH-36 heating element.

TOOLS

Woodcarving, woodworking, machine, and hand tools are available at hardware and art supply stores.

Charles T. Bainbridge's Sons
20 Cumberland Street
Brooklyn, New York 11205
 Keeton Kutter: instant mat cutter. Keeton Mat Marker: layout mats before cutting. Keeton Cardboard & Glass Kutter. Also supplies other tools and findings in addition to a full range of mats and backings.

Blank-It Corporation
P.O. Box 569
309 West Crowell Street
Monroe, N.C. 28110
 FRAME-UP!: a picture frame construction device that adjusts to support frames up to 48".

Peter Brunger Product Development
300 E. Fulton
Grand Rapids, Mich. 49502
 ANKER EDGE mat cutter, in stainless steel or aluminum in different lengths. Comes with a Cuta-mat bevel knife that has an angles wheel on one side.

CCM Arts & Crafts, Inc.
9520 Baltimore Avenue
College Park, Md. 20740
 Bevel mat cutter.

C. S. Osborne Tool Company
125 Jersey Street
Harrison, N.J. 07029
 Knives and other carving and cutting tools.

Stanley Tools
New Britain, Conn.
 Stanley Mitre Machine, Stanley Joining Vise, and a full range of wood, metal, and plastic-working tools.

Universal Clamp Corp.
6905 Cedros Avenue
Van Nuys, Calif. 91405
 Universal clamp.

Henry Westpfal & Co., Inc.
4 E. 32nd Street
New York, N.Y. 10016
 General tools and supplies.

X-Acto Precision Tools, Inc.
48—41 Van Dam Street
Long Island City, N.Y. 11101
 Knives.

INDEX